Adventures in Leanland

Lean people in lean businesses in a lean, mean world

Russell Watkins

Published in the United Kingdom by:

Lean Sempai Publishing
Ashbourne
Derbyshire
info@sempai.co.uk

Content copyright © Russell Watkins, 2011

All rights reserved. No portion of this book may be reproduced, stored in a retrieval system or transmitted at any time or by any means mechanical, electronic, photocopying, recording or otherwise, without the prior, written permission of the publisher.

The right of Russell Watkins to be identified as the author of this work has been asserted by him in accordance with the Copyright, Designs and Patents act 1988.

A CIP record of this book is available from the British Library.

First printed 2011

ISBN 978-0-9570595-0-4

Cover design by design wall limited www.designwall.co.uk

TABLE OF CONTENTS

Acknowledgements

Preface

Chapter 1: The Lean World - Challenges for modern manufacturing

"A frog in a well knows not the ocean"

1.1 We all have our cross to bear   3
1.2 The "Western" response   6
1.3 The "Eastern" Challenge   9
1.4 Adapt & survive   13

Chapter 2: The Lean World - 6 keys to survival

"The rain falls, the ground hardens"

2.1 Key 1 - Seeing clearly   17
2.2 Key 2 - Building good people to build good products   20
2.3 Key 3 - Turning complexity into simplicity   26
2.4 Key 4 - Man v machine: The automation conundrum   29
2.5 Key 5 - One or Many: The sourcing conundrum   32
2.6 Key 6 - Education, Education, Education   35
2.7 In conclusion   37

Chapter 3: The Lean Business - Practical ways to deal with a crisis

"Which will prevail, the rabbit or the fox?"

3.1 What kind of fool would create a crisis?   41
3.2 Anyone can look...few can see   43
3.3 Deckchairs on the Titanic   45
3.4 Dealing with Material and Labour cost pain   47
3.5 Fight the fight at the right enemy   52

Chapter 4: The Lean Business - Is this a walk through a great factory?

"Lipstick on a pig"

4.1 A virtual walk through a lean Factory   57
4.2 Brief encounter   59
4.3 Shipping dock, Customer delivery & finished goods warehouse   61
4.4 The Assembly area   63
4.5 In-house component manufacturing   67
4.6 Material delivery & goods inwards   69

Chapter 5: The Lean Business - 'Kodawari' means 'attention to detail'

"Snipers, cyclists and mechanics"

5.1 Tri, tri and tri again   75
5.2 Sky is the limit   77
5.3 Cyclists and cricketers   80
5.4 Kodawari and lean   84
5.5 One hour and seventeen minutes   92
5.6 Control - and kodawari - before kaizen   97

Chapter 6: The Lean You - Flexibility

"The mighty oak or the flexible reed"

6.1 The sustainability key – lean leadership   105
6.2 The silent flute   111
6.3 Scenario 1: Walk a while in another man's shoes   113
6.4 Scenario 2: Catch many small fish, not one big one   119
6.5 Scenario 3: A chick waiting for a worm   125
6.6 Scenario 4: The map is not the territory   129
6.7 Scenario 5: The answer's no, now what's the question?   132
6.8 To a man with a hammer, everything looks like a nail   137

Chapter 7: The Lean You - Clear Thinking

"Time is the shadow of motion"

7.1 The T in TPS also stands for thinking   143

7.2 Challenge yourself   146
7.3 Not all work is valuable   148
7.4 Snatching defeat from the jaws of victory   152

Chapter 8: The Lean You - Personal responsibility

"It's difficult to wake someone who is pretending to be asleep"

8.1 Sensei, Sempai, Kohai   169
8.2 Rugby, rules and TCUP   172
8.3 In the lean environment   176

Chapter 9: The Sensei view - Reflections of a Toyota veteran

"He who chops his own wood warms himself twice"

9.1 On...working at Toyota in the 1960's   183
9.2 On...training at Toyota   186
9.3 On...consultants and the Management responsibility   190
9.4 On...the future   194

A Final Word   199

With grateful thanks to my three mentors, in order of our first meeting

Toshiyuki 'Mick' Muraoka
Mark Hayward
Alan Blake

Passionate and practical leaders, clear and deep thinkers.

Doris, thanks for equipping me so well for the journey.

Steph, Millie and Archie - it's all about you.

Preface

"Leanland" is a place that cannot be found on any map. In times long since past, "leanland" was situated almost exclusively within the well-guarded borders of the manufacturing sector. Today we are all, like it or not, citizens of leanland. Even if you do not ply your trade directly within manufacturing, sectors like financial services have come on board in recent years. Government at all levels, in countries scattered across the globe, are having their heads turned by the attractive 'greater bang for each Government buck' prospect that lean provides in these cash-strapped times.

The unrelenting need is to square the daunting circle of cost-cutting to deliver public services without degrading the provision and quality of those front line services. Lean is plan A, plan B and plan C and there is no way back. "Lean Healthcare" is firmly embedded into the Government lexicon in the UK and the US where we witness an Obama administration regularly using the language of lean.

Collectively it is time for us to surrender to the lean revolution (about time, this particular revolution has had 500 years to take hold!). At the risk of sounding apocalyptic, our not too distant future offers the prospect of wars fought over the human staples of water, food security and, barring enormous levels of technological innovation, scarcity across the board. Now is the time to curtail our wasteful ways.

Here endeth the sermon, save to say; if you are alive today, you are a citizen of leanland by default. Lean is the only viable game in town as we venture into a New (resource starved) World where our ships have been scuttled for us, Cortes style.

The world needs many things; cures for persistent diseases, the resolution of destructive conflicts unsettling entire regions, the ending of poverty driving humanitarian crises on a massive scale. What it doesn't need is another book. And yet, here for your consideration, I present another book.

"Adventures in Leanland" is my way of helping to prepare for the journey. Type any combination of book titles involving the magic word "lean" into Amazon and you'll get upwards of 48,000 results. The odds appear to be stacked against me. I've read a few of those 48,000 books and browsed a great many others, sacrificing valuable hours that I'll never get back. Some are excellent, informative and entertaining. Most are dry, essentially inaccessible and written in an academic prose that tends to be impenetrable.

The premise of this book is simple. To survive, each of us needs to become a lean person operating in a lean organisation prospering in a lean, but mean, world. This book shines some light into the dark corners where our collective challenges lurk. 'Adventures in Leanland' will let daylight in upon magic to look at the essential requirements of a lean organisation and thoroughly explore the personal qualities you'll need to prosper into the future.

This book, I hope, strikes a balance by conveying useful, practical information in a lively way. I'd like to pass on some of the knowledge I have gained from excellent mentors and hands-on effort in some very fine lean companies, but I'd also like you to enjoy the ride. I am fortunate to have passed through the doorways of over a hundred businesses around the world. Mostly I have managed to evade the bland temptations of the "royal tour" to observe, prod and poke the real underbelly of these businesses; the light and dark which so clearly illuminates their remarkable similarities and fascinating differences.

Once upon a time in Mexico, I was greeted and seriously 'powerpointed' in the office of the Managing Director, prior to learning a good deal more about the company during subsequent lunch breaks. Breaks that were, at the invitation of a Team Leader, happily passed in the back yard of the factory seeing how long I could hold onto a couple of electrodes hastily wired up to a car battery. This standard breaktime practice fades slowly from the mind, as does the mocking laughter of a dozen sinewy Mexicans. Shaking and weeping to one side, I became an accepted, albeit temporary, member of the team at that exact point...and I learned a little about the culture...and I got to see how the yard and the external logistics were managed.

In South America, I have marvelled at the unrivalled dexterity of Peruvian Windscreen assemblers in Lima, spinning windscreens like gifted extras in a Samurai movie. In Kobe, Japan, minutes of my life were lost as I became absorbed trying to figure out why the man in front of me was repeatedly tapping torqued nuts with a toffee hammer before listening intently for the pitch of the metallic reply. The privilege of witnessing a coconut based ceremony, to bless the opening of a new production line in Pune, India stays with me to this day. Closer to home, I recall the pitying glances of co-workers as I inadvertently stopped the moving assembly line whilst trying to understand and copy the knacks involved in assembling an air conditioning unit. Knacks imperceptible to the casual eye, yet balletic in their dexterity.

In short, I have been lucky to experience many things. The chapters that follow are full of examples, specific advice, lean teaching and stories from leanland and beyond. Whilst there is, unmistakably, a Japanese perspective at work between these covers (unsurprising, as I was initially trained by a Japanese Toyota master engineer and have spent much of the last 4 years consulting to a Toyota group company) I have worked hard to keep it in check. This book is not 'Zen and the art of Lean Management' in disguise. It is, I believe, deeply practical.

The idea for this book grew out of a series of very well received, but not widely distributed, articles I wrote for an institute in the UK. The penning of these articles was enjoyable, if time consuming. This book is a result of my reasoning that I'd already eaten the poison, so might as well lick the plate and write a whole book.

Of course, my hope is that you enjoy the read, but please let me know if you think I've missed the point somewhere. Because the contents are original, in that they are the structured ramblings of a veteran lean queen, you may not agree with everything. This is as it should be. Feel free to open up a conversation with me via russell@sempai.co.uk to improve our mutual understanding. My fundamental aim is for you to find much in here that makes you go "ah, that's what it means" or "that's a good idea". So, take what you like and leave the rest.

Chapter 1

The Lean World - Challenges for modern manufacturing

"A frog in a well knows not the ocean"

1.1 We all have our cross to bear

Power in the manufacturing world has been generally migrating east for some time. China, India, Russia and Brazil (the former two tend to attract the attention, but all four have been on the move) are shaping up to be economic powerhouses for generations to come. Their specific advantage to date has been an extremely low labour cost driven by a huge labour pool. Economic prosperity has been concentrated, (Beijing and Shanghai together house an estimated 18,000 individuals worth more than 10 million US Dollars each!) but continues to spread from coastal areas up along the rivers inland. In China, even now, close to a billion people live on less than $2 a day.

Five years ago, in the construction industry alone, Indian labour was one-tenth of the UK labour cost, China one-fifteenth. True enough, wages are on the rise but these gaps are not diminishing as rapidly as hoped. In a manufacturing sense, these countries have thus far advanced to the point of primarily producing commodities. This is a natural growth path and, at first glance, a wise move in a world where more and more items are becoming commodities.

The prime drawback of an entirely commodity-driven economy is the tendency to compete on price alone. No major industrial nation has become so with a low wage economy at its foundations. China and India understand that the low-wage advantage is time limited. They realise that a nation with increasing wages and comparable living standards to the western world is not developed by making and exporting cheap commodities. They are making significant progress and are geared up to respond to the stark fact that, with few exceptions, todays value-added quickly becomes tomorrow's commodity.

China shares a troubled history with its close neighbour Japan that colours relations to this day, yet the stark economic fact is that China's labour cost is a fraction of Japan's. Increasingly, it can produce good quality products at a lower cost in areas where Japan and the West have transferred technical know-how, hired local people, bought machines and trained them. The same has happened in Malaysia, South Korea and Thailand. The Thai supply chain, flood risk excepted, has in no small part been developed by Japanese companies like Toyota.

The ticket to the big game is to become an economy that creates intellectual property. Wages are continuing to rise steadily in these economies: a manageable situation when your customers are experiencing a seemingly endless up cycle in their economies. Prolonged global recession, like the one that we have recently experienced, prompts some interesting reactions, not least of all the returning spectre of protectionism brought about by Western Europeans and Americans suffering domestic job losses.

This is why China and India, not to mention Thailand and Vietnam, are beginning to move up the supply chain into more value-added products like subassembly, systems supply, sequenced supply and design collaboration. In any event, most of us globally are preoccupied with migrating up the supply chain closer to the OEMs and the ultimate consumer.

Established Western manufacturing businesses have scratched their heads hard to create workable strategies catering for a global spread of factories. Large OEMs are often committed to building locally to sell locally. This means final assembly plants in far-flung corners of the world with relatively stable political bases, agricultural societies, and a ready labour pool with the right demographic attributes – although they may well need training – close to deep water ports and so on.

There have been many serious capital commitments in developing economies with real intent to build a skills base and the quality consciousness required to maintain global standards. Strength has permeated through Eastern supply chains as they begin to grasp the exacting demands of a Toyota or a Honda. The Thai supply chain in particular is gaining a reputation as a strong supply base, with many suppliers capable of meeting demanding Japanese quality requirements and standards.

1.2 The "Western Response"

What is our collective western response to this surge? It varies. If you are a parent shopping for toys, t-shirts or electronic goods, there are reasons to be cheerful... notwithstanding the concerns of maltreatment of workers in some factories and lower tier suppliers occasionally circumnavigating the technical manufacturing specification – think lead paint being licked from cheap toys by gleeful infants.

Interestingly, even those of us who are aware of the troubling reports of appalling conditions, and surging suicide rates, in corners of developing economies soon forget this when faced with a cheap pair of jeans in our local supermarket. Conscience, it seems, has a time and a place.

At a business level, the understandable reflex for many manufacturers in the west is to feel threatened, because low-cost economies mean we have to compete harder to overcome the direct labour cost disadvantage. There is, though, a churlishness to our looking east with bitterness and begrudging others their time in the sun. After all, in economic terms the 19th Century belonged to Britain, the 20th century to the US. Things change as things always change. It looks very much as though the 21st century will belong to Asia.

The response required is something different. I am reminded of the story (recounted by Joe Hyams in his superb book "Zen in the Martial Arts") of the Buddhist master who, whilst guiding a student, drew a line on the floor with a piece chalk and then asked the student:

'How can you make this line shorter?'

The student studied the line and gave a few suggestions, most involving cutting the line into smaller pieces. The Master shook his head and drew a second, longer, line on the floor next to it, before asking:

'How does the first line look now?'

'Shorter,' came the sheepish reply.

Our focus must be on making our line longer and improving our competitiveness (see chapters 3, 4 and 5) before rushing for the familiar comfort of protectionist trade policies historically favoured by some nations. The US and France in particular, whilst being enthusiastic exponents, have experienced a singular lack of success from following this insular path. It is hard to conclude anything beyond the long-proven need to trade with the world to survive.

Take the example of Japan again, which comprises a series of islands with perilously few natural resources. It is forced to import over 95% of its oil, gas and steel, and has, through necessity, developed a naturally frugal mindset. Indeed, this lack of resources paved the way for the nightmare scenario realised in 2011 by the Japanese Tsunami. A lack of choices, not desire, leads a small country like Japan to decide to build 50+ nuclear power plants at the meeting point of three of our more capricious tectonic plates.

In such a culture, Waste elimination is not a nice-to-have activity confined to occasional improvement efforts on the shop floor. You tend to become good at the things you have to become good at to survive – or you don't survive. This predisposition to squeezing every last drop or ounce out of a resource has been aptly described as 'wringing water out of dry towels'. Speaking practically, this means using labour effectively, not making bad quality goods, not allowing machines to leak, taking only one paper towel (after washing your hands) in a restaurant rather than a handful. Japan is only one of a number of countries lacking an abundance of natural resources. Bountiful nations, like those in Western Europe, will struggle to develop a dogged resistance to wastefulness and a collectively frugal mindset that informs a thousand simple activities every day.

In these days of carbon footprints and dwindling natural resources, can you think of a greater crime than adding value to a product only to scrap it late on in the production process? It is no accident that Japanese car manufacturers are generally the most productive and cost-effective in the world. They had no choice in a nation of few natural resources scarred by the atomic end to the Second World War.

Another positive response is for us in 'the west' to understand our other competitive advantage. Geographically, our proximity to wealthy consumers better places us to understand their needs and develop products they want. The way to do this, and our challenge in the UK, is to make and design things – in a cost-effective way – that people want to buy. In other words, innovate, compete on value-added and deliver consistent top-notch quality from a trusted brand.

1.3 The "Eastern" Challenge

The global challenge for emerging nations is a more basic one of creating an infrastructure to support economic development. Two of the fundamental needs remain, as they always have, to get goods to market and people to work. The infrastructure to satisfy these needs is forming at different rates in India and China, both of whom have also been developing quality consciousness.

In the more developed parts of India, the condition and partially organised chaos of major roads in and around cities such as Delhi, Mumbai and Pune take some getting used to. The average vehicle speed in India is 25mph and there is still much work for them to do to develop the smooth infrastructure we take for granted in western economies. Yet many Indian plants manage to run JIT supply operations with lean inventory supply chains. Equally, don't be fooled into thinking that these are uneducated people. Indian engineers are some of the most creative, not to mention hardworking, at developing low-cost solutions to complex problems. India boasts an educational system that turns out huge number of graduates every year into a culture where higher education is prized. Some of the best manufacturing plants I have spent time in are located around Delhi and compare favourably to anything I have seen on four continents.

The fifth continent, Africa, is an enigma wrapped in a mystery. How will the African conundrum finally be resolved? A continent which, if political, religious and economic stability allows could become an 'African Union' of a size and strength to rival all-comers. China, alive to this opportunity, is pumping billions of dollars into the dark continent in anticipation of socio-political-economic benefits in years to come. China has the patience and arguable power of a nation with huge foreign currency reserves. This is, of course, a simplistic assessment of the way of things, but we do have a simple choice of trying to cut their line or lengthen our own. In fact, our lines are inextricably linked. Several years ago the London uber-rich hailed from Russia, now many are Chinese.

China herself has experienced growing pains. Cities like Beijing are plagued by polluting smog. The three rivers dam project will have reverberations for many generations to come. Coal-fired power stations have been opening in China every 10 days for several years. Twenty nuclear power stations are planned to come on-stream in the next three years. A proportion of this is a natural by-product of the rapid industrialisation of a society. Frighteningly, though, a third of China's double-digit percentage annual GDP growth is generated by cleaning up after the other two thirds of true economic growth.

China also has a reputation problem. The economy is often accused of the theft of ideas from 'the west'. Persistent, often merited, accusations of copying to produce items as diverse as grey market car spares, designer shoes and memory sticks at a fraction of western market prices is endemic. The Shanghai 'copy' market, for example, is not a covert operation. When I visited (purely to browse in the name of research), it operated from a permanent home underneath a museum. It has and is proving very difficult to protect ideas and intellectual capital from reverse engineering.

Japan is an interesting example of a nation that prides itself, to a degree, on its ability to imitate and leapfrog; in other words, to take what is being done elsewhere and make it better. Beyond semantics, this is different from copying as it perpetuates intellectual capital.

More prosaically, getting goods to market and people to work usually requires roads. Thousands of roads need to be built throughout India, China, Brazil and right across the continent of Africa. This need drives a requirement for construction equipment such as excavators and diggers. Once built, cars and other smaller vehicles make use of the roads to move the people and goods around.

Let us take a closer look then at the automotive and off-highway (construction equipment) OEM manufacturers who would be at the centre of this advancement, to glean an interesting perspective on globalisation. Ironically, a significant part of the solution for many western manufacturers has been to source from these low, euphemistically named 'best', cost economies (if we make the naively generous assumption that all of the off-shoring maths has been done correctly).

Fabrications, castings or component parts with a high manual content are often sourced abroad; these being the items that can be made cheaply overseas and nested in shipping containers for cost-effective transport back to final assembly plants in Europe and the US, for example.

Back in 2007, Dan Jones wrote a fairly innocuous but excellent article dissecting the true 'maths' of off-shoring. The article peeled back onion-like layers of cost to reveal a plethora of costs way beyond simplistic piece-part comparisons. At that point insufficient numbers of purchasing professionals paid heed. Today, the off-shoring counter-revolution (on-shoring) gathers a head of steam. On-shoring driven by the three-headed beast of (a) tardy recognition of the true cost and management pain involved in managing extended supply chains established in a hurry (b) finally doing the maths correctly when the actual numbers didn't add up, and (c) rising labour costs in developing countries.

A glamorous roll-call of companies headed by the likes of Toyota, GM,

Honda, JCB and Caterpillar took tentative steps over the years and built fabrication plants in developing countries. Sensibly, they took the brave second step of establishing final assembly capability in these countries to avoid an intractable problem that forces its way to the surface if emerging economies are exploited purely as commodity sweatshops.

To understand this problem, imagine the life of an excavator. It is made by cutting up thick sheets of steel and bending, machining and welding them together to make sub-assemblies. These are then welded together into larger modules of the excavator and have a cab, engine, transmission and attachments, not to mention thousands of other, smaller parts bolted to them. It makes sense to do a fair proportion of the cutting, bending, drilling and subassembly welding (pre-paint) in low-cost economies. These sub-assemblies can then be sent back to European or US factories for final weld, paint and final assembly.

The excavator is finished, gleaming and ready for shipment to – you guessed it – India or China or Russia or Brazil to build roads! If you ship an excavator, you ship a good deal of expensive fresh air. The long-term solution has been to move the overseas fabrication plants away from a staple purely of fabrication and into final assembly.

1.4   Adapt & Survive

In other words, source globally and final assemble locally, wherever the demand justifies it. The phrase 'wherever the demand justifies it' raises the issue of global capacity management. Demand patterns ebb and flow over time both in volume and mix. The smart businesses think of ways to manage capacity globally to be able to move work from factory to factory in response to changing customer patterns.

To turn capacity on and off or at least flex the variants being made, you need to be able to guarantee the same level of quality across the entire business. This means establishing a common quality standard worldwide with the same high degree of process control and supplier management. This in turn requires high levels of skill, control and quality consciousness locally.

Couple this with the demands on management back at base to bridge a vast span of control to keep information – think engineering design changes, cut-ins, spreading best practice, resolving quality issues – and materials flowing rapidly and efficiently around the globe. Managing engineering changes is a big enough challenge, without the vexing complication of communicating across cultures and languages over long distances. A complication multiplied many-fold by New Product Introduction (NPI).

It is reckoned, by minds finer than mine, that there are four factors to securing a successful product launch:

- Get what people want
- Get it to market quickly
- Do it with a small number of engineering hours

- Make the product inherently makeable and kaizen-able

The big three US automakers probably compete with Toyota at a plant level, but the difference is in the lean design, the product development, purchasing system and management attitude. So, how do you guarantee quality and delivery of current and new products – to keep the brand trusted! – with a workforce finding its manufacturing feet in factories thousands of miles from the warm bosom of HQ? Ex-farmers are assembling engines and gearboxes in China and India as we speak.

These are the questions that, all being well, keep your CEOs awake at night pacing the floor in an effort to provide workable answers. It is in these dark lonely hours that a CEO truly earns his or her handsome remuneration package.

The next chapter shifts from the global and general to draw out six of the more specific challenges together with some fascinating examples.

Chapter 2

The Lean World - 6 keys to survival

"The rain falls, the ground hardens"

2.1 Key 1 - Seeing Clearly

The lean gurus of my generation, Womack and Jones, will argue that any organisation needs purpose, process and people. For a manufacturing business the purpose of existence is to prosper by performing value creating activities to solve its customers' problems. There are broadly three processes that achieve these aims: (i) Design (ii) Fulfil – that is, make something and (iii) Sustain – help the end customer use, over time, whatever it is you have sold them.

People come into play because we drive our business forward by engaging everyone who touches any of these three processes in looking for ways to improve it. The natural and implicit extension of this statement is to question why, if you have people who do not touch a value creating process, do you have these people at all?

A depressingly small proportion of the top automakers, aerospace and off-highway construction companies have clear purpose and good eyesight. Strategically, they look far into the future to try to solve tomorrow's problems today. Environmental far-sightedness in the last decade has fuelled the push to make the hybrid car a viable option. Clear vision and strong leadership – by setting seemingly impossible internal targets – pushed engineers within companies like Honda and Toyota to do what needed to be done: challenge fixed ideas.

The polarisation of the two giants in aircraft manufacture, Boeing and Airbus, is another fascinating example. Both have bet the house on diametrically opposed strategies for aircraft size and range based on totally different beliefs as to how customers will prefer to fly in the future.

Airbus has created the A380 to support the hub-and-spoke system where customers are routed in a network through one or two major hubs – for example, Chicago, Houston or Hong Kong. Boeing, with its Dreamliner, predicts a stronger move towards faster direct flights without the need to route through a hub. Both have clear vision: but which, if either, is looking in the right direction?

Let us turn back to Toyota briefly. Notwithstanding it's well documented recall problems of the last two years (John Shook and Jeffrey Liker have both written very clearly and level headedly about this) Toyota patiently cultivated the advantage of excellent business processes to organise production, product development, supplier management and people development. They have had the tricky work of creating and integrating processes that, at their stage of maturity, are robust enough to be transplanted to new countries.

Although Toyota still feels the need to send out seasoned co-ordinators from Japan to support overseas plants, this is for a critical but less tangible reason. It is not to fix or compensate for broken processes, but to help establish new plants and then focus on teaching the Toyota Way to local management. Understanding and living the Toyota Way generates Toyota results.

If you give a man a fish, you feed him for a day. Teach him how to fish...well you know how this hackneyed, yet resolutely sound, quotation concludes. These co-ordinators are vastly experienced teachers whose job goes way beyond teaching processes into teaching management how to teach, coach and manage as if they had no authority; to instil an understanding that my job is not to do my job, but to IMPROVE the way I do my job. This is part of the reason why even Toyota's most experienced co-ordinator will never claim fully to understand TPS. A system that has people at the centre, more specifically, respect for people, takes many years to bear good fruit. To bear good fruit repeatedly, a tree requires sufficient watering and selective pruning.

2.2 Key 2 - Building good people to build good products

People, and respect for people, are very much in evidence in the approach to leadership of world class manufacturers; an approach which is fascinating but not well understood by many. The essence of learning at these world class businesses is that you earn knowledge through developing a questioning mind, keen senses and dirty fingernails. The good coach creates the right environment and asks the right reflective questions, but never directly reveals the path (see chapter 6 on Flexibility for five great stories on exactly this subject). The path is often tough for us to follow, as it is full of subtleties and takes time to tread.

Taking time is not something we generally applaud in the west. Mastery of an art, however, is driven by repeated practice and a focus on the process. If one eye is impatiently fixed upon the destination, there is only one eye left to find the way. Life would indeed be much simpler if our Manager/coach just told us the answer to a question. This does not build for the future and will not foster people who are engaged in their work or build strong team leaders, strong supervisors and strong managers.

There is a phrase in Japanese – *Monozukuri wa hito zukuri* – the essence of which is to build good people to build good products. Good people are not built by gifting them knowledge. How many of us, as children, learn that a hot iron should not be touched? Surely it should be enough for our mother to warn us. I'll raise a mildly scarred hand into the air here to concede that, in my case, being told a great many things was rarely enough. How many of us gained confidence solely by being told that we are capable of riding a bike? Riding the bike – and falling off it occasionally – builds skill, experience and the confidence to encourage others into the saddle.

The manifestation of this inherent coaching culture is that such companies want their managers to say neither 'Do it like this' nor 'Do it your way', but 'Follow me and we're going to figure this out together'. 'Lead the organisation as if you have no power' is the oft-quoted mantra. Each level of management must visualise the problems for people to get to work on them.

One of the reasons why better manufacturing businesses have a healthier ratio of team leaders to direct associates, than supervisors to team leaders, is the belief that the team leader role goes beyond the vague idea of keeping an eye on the troops and process practiced by most. Their belief is that improvements are made, costs are reduced and the timeline is reduced by empowering many people to solve many small problems at the lowest level in the business.

Thus, team leaders and supervisors spend their day confirming the process – think area patrols and check sheets – and trying to get to the root cause of problems by running small PDCA trials. 'We haven't got time for this' is the response from a typical UK manufacturer.

Consider the statistic that roughly 70% of a typical team leader's – unstructured! – working day is spent doing two things: hunting for parts and deciding what to make next. The better manufacturing companies have freed up some of this 70% by developing lean material supply systems – internal and external logistics – and using simple levelling and pull mechanisms to make the decision of what to make next very clear.

The void created by eliminating this wasteful work should be then filled quickly with structured work: process confirmation, responding to andons, problem-solving, and promoting kaizen for example.

So, 'respect for people' involves training and encouraging people to visualise and solve problems. Once again, we come back to the process. The question is not who was to blame, but what in the process was not robust enough to make it impossible to make a mistake.

Jidoka or autonomation – automation with a human touch – is one of the pillars of the Toyota house. It promotes both quality and respect for people. Jidoka has several meanings, but essentially it is the ability to separate the man and the machine. Sakichi Toyoda's automated loom, which stopped itself when a thread broke, thus avoiding the wastage of a poor garment, was initially a productivity boon. It also, more notably, gave rise to the idea of building in quality, not merely inspecting it in. This great industrial shift in labour productivity promoted greater respect for people as asking a person to watch a machine, in case it goes wrong, clearly has no respect for the abilities of that person – beyond the innate ability to see!

Quality consciousness has again moved on with the development of Jikoutei-Kanketsu (Built-in Quality with Ownership); a practical, deeply integrated approach to the paradox at the core of Quality. If Quality IS everyone's responsibility, as received wisdom tells us, then precisely what should I do as an individual? Everything? Something? If the answer is 'something', what precisely should that something be if I am an Industrial Engineer or a Buyer or a Materials Controller?

The Jikoutei-Kanketsu approach to Quality is one of those open secrets at the heart of TPS whereby the entire product development lifecycle from concept to cut-in, and beyond, are considered. For this book, we'll limit ourselves to Jidoka.

Before a discussion of the machine side of Jidoka, let's consider people again. Jidoka refers not only to process error-proofing, but also to empowering people to stop the line when they spot an abnormality or problem and find out what has gone wrong, to get to the root cause and prevent recurrence. A problem, tightly defined in this scenario, being anything that deviates away from the standard. The line worker uses an andon to get the attention of his team leader quickly when a problem occurs.

Quickly refers not only to the speed of recognising a problem, but also the speed of getting to the scene. Ask any detective how important it is to get to the crime scene whilst the body is warm and nothing has been touched. The andon pull may or may not stop the line based on the response time and diagnosis of the team leader.

In actuality, most final assembly plants operate fixed position stops and buffer parts of the track to minimise disruption. Very few factories – and most of those that do are Japanese – actually empower people to stop their own work and the work of those around them. What is the rationale for doing such a counterintuitive thing? The answer; stopping for a few seconds now is cheaper, safer and better for quality than reworking later.

Imagine the quality risk and cost of stripping and reassembling a car in a corner of the factory to get to a small internal component that has failed. Let's make the heroic assumption that you have been lucky and the problem affects just the one car (more likely hundreds) by the time you find it. Even if you 'solve' the problem through rework, how do you know you've rebuilt it correctly to spec? If we rely primarily on the end of line inspector, value has been added to the bad part from fabrication process or supplier, so that the scrap cost now equals labour cost + the cost of the other good parts assembled to it. Feedback from end-of-line inspection is too late, not dissimilar to using a post mortem to advise someone to stop smoking.

Finally, rework is not good for morale long term. We could debate the short-term benefits of sustained overtime, but suffice to say that this has both a business and personal cost; and shows a fundamental disrespect for people as rework is clearly wasteful work.

One word in the preceding section should be stressed: abnormality. A prerequisite to using andon successfully and building in quality is spotting abnormalities. However, to spot what is abnormal we have to define what is normal. Organising your working environment and processes sufficiently to make clear what is normal takes dedication and control. Hence, the culture of stop, call, wait – stop if you see a problem, call your team leader and wait for them to arrive – is claimed by many but truly pursued by few. In their most fundamental forms, 5s, Standardised Work and Visual Factory exist to make abnormality clear to us, quickly.

A good example of the depth of andon was reported in the news recently. A leading Japanese auto plant in the US reports 2,000 separate andon pulls per month; meaning that, on 2,000 occasions in the month, a succession of individuals spotted a potential problem. By contrast, in the same period, a similar sized new plant run by one of the top three big US auto car companies had two andon pulls. Ask yourself which you consider to be the better line? Is a line without interruptions a good or bad line? This innocuous question cuts to the very heart of lean.
The lean view is that a smooth running line is a lazy line in which we are clearly not engaging our people to find opportunities to improve. This 'better is not good enough' approach stems from a different attitude to problems. If problems are viewed as opportunities and we empower people to find them – and to tell us when they've found them – we send a better product into the market place at a lower cost. We also respect our

people for the brains they have.

This relentlessly restless approach is neatly summed up as 'no problem is a problem'. To be able to identify and solve a problem, you therefore have to have a standard against which to compare. This applies to any and all parts of the business. In a purely manufacturing sense, it reaches all the way back to the basics of ensuring that an associate on the shopfloor has a robust process and standardised work to follow; as well as the correct materials, training, etc.

A world class manufacturer also excels at setting up a robust process, standardising it and CONTINUOUSLY confirming that the process is running as expected. If it is, the aim is to improve it in small ways daily; if it isn't, find the problem and prevent its recurrence. Whilst people undeniably need training and coaching to support this approach, successful exemplars are spread across the globe. A popular quotation in relation to Toyota is that they have 'ordinary people running extraordinary processes' rather than the more popular way of finding 'gifted people to run broken processes'.

2.3 Key 3 - Turning complexity into simplicity

The task in any manufacturing business, big or small, is to take the complex problems and create simple solutions that are repeatable irrespective of the person performing the task. Once again, the objective is to make it easy to do the right thing. Exporting broken processes around the world is unlikely to work, no matter how gifted the people you hire... oh, and gifted people are less available and more costly.

Of course, we cannot rely solely on people. Not all problems can be seen: lines run quickly, especially when a line is running to 50-second takt time; and people can inadvertently create problems by picking the wrong parts, fitting them the wrong way round or not tightening them enough. We can reduce the risk and impact of human errors by having good 5S, creating strong, living standardised work and introducing robust neighbour checks. This will not guarantee our goal of zero defects.

Thankfully, many enlightened plants have now realised that placing an inspector at the end of the line serves to inflate both cost and lead time. The knock-out blow to this double-whammy is that it stealthily takes away the incentive to improve our process. An end-of-line inspector is also subject to the same human frailties as those who build the product before the inspector sees it. Of course, in a lean sense, picking the wrong parts, fitting them the wrong way round or not tightening them enough are failures of the process, not the people. People will always make mistakes because, well, they're people. Our aim, realistically, is to maximise the interval between mistakes whilst ensuring that our firewalls prevent defects flowing out to the Customer. Understanding quality assurance means understanding the difference between occurrence prevention and flow-out prevention. Indeed, if we are serious about PDCA, our firewalls themselves should change in terms of position, size and composition of checks over time.

We need to error-proof the process – the machines, jigs and fixtures – to make it easy to do the right thing. Error-proofing, at best, means small, inexpensive mechanical devices. Out of necessity it is sometimes more complex; for example, pick-by-light systems that ensure that the right variant of a part is chosen and fitted. Fitting an airbag in a car, by necessity, relies on picking systems, bar coding, torque and angle monitoring and recording because of legislative safety requirements.

At worst, error-proofing is overcomplicated, hard to maintain, inflexible and packed with so many bells and whistles that it is prone to failure or misjudgement. Such devices are easy to spot as operators have generally had to find a way to trick or override the error-proof to maintain some semblance of productivity and flow. A problematic solution, true enough, but also a useful indicator that we have got our engineering wrong. To see simple, elegant, mechanical devices in operation, lay your hands on a karakuri doll. These Japanese dolls date back hundreds of years and use simple mechanical devices to move and perform articulated movements that we now rely on microchips to produce.

Over-complication has become fashionable recent years where the mantra of more choice is warmly embraced as, without exception, being a good thing. Beware any rule that has no exceptions. The market place demands that we offer 15 different shades of this or 20 slightly different sizes of the other...or does it. False proliferation, not driven by customer demand but by sales and marketing or designer whim, has become very popular. The Industrial Engineering, Bill of Materials and Logistics impact of "just one more part number" are startling.

Of course, the situation had to improve from fifteen years ago when, for example, construction customers were merely happy to receive a digger that worked most of the time. Today, they demand this as a given and want an aesthetic finish comparable to a family car. Mass customisation, coupled with higher quality demands, means that we present the people building our products with a dazzling range of opportunities to get it wrong.

Think again about globalisation and new overseas plants staffed with people unfamiliar with our products or manufacturing in any sense. Asking someone to remember and visually check 14 different attributes within a 50-second takt time is a ludicrous proposition. Even if we find someone who can, what happens when that person is ill, takes holidays or decides to leave our business?

This scenario of 14 checks in 50 seconds is an example of one of the 3Ms: Muda (waste), Mura (unevenness; a lack of levelling) and Muri. Muri relates to overburden. It can be manifested as asking a machine to run too fast, a crane to pick up too much or a person to do too much. In a nine-hour shift, at a 50-second takt time, an operator would process 600 parts. Fourteen attributes per part would equal 8,000 checks per day.

Most people reading this book will encounter a low energy point in the day where concentration falters. It is, however, feasible to teach two or three checks and ask the process to do the rest. As we indicated earlier, there really is no long-term sustainable alternative to built-in quality.

2.4 Key 4 - Man v machine: The automation conundrum

The message, as with much in life, is all things in moderation. An over-reliance on technology is as bad as an under-reliance. Above all, we must keep it simple. A classic case in point was the costly, heavily automated new GM/Cadillac plant opened in the US in the 1980's. Reports quickly emerged that robots designed to spray cars were spraying each other, a robot built to install windscreens was smashing them and complex materials systems were bedevilled by glitches. Much of the unnecessary automation was taken out and the plant won awards five or six years later.

There are two points to be made here. Firstly, automate where you <u>have to</u>, for safety, quality or competitive advantage reasons such as labour cost, not just where you can. I'll say it again; an over-reliance on technology is as bad as under-reliance. Secondly, if you do automate, keep it simple and flexible to embrace the need to change.

The fashionable lean tool of the noughties decade, value stream mapping (VSM), takes us into the exciting flow world of heijunka and kanban. Many industrial engineers with whom I have worked suffer from a natural overcomplication of simple solutions and an aversion to basic improvement techniques in favour of the sexy ones. At its base, VSM has process stability; have you got enough trained men to do the work, enough materials on hand to meet today's requirements, a robust method to combine the two and machines with sufficient availability and flexibility to keep running.

A well designed kanban system cannot function if the machines required to produce parts cannot do so quickly enough. Indeed, one of Toyota's hidden strengths is its' approach to automation, maintenance and jig, tool and die design. This competence was, once again, driven by necessity. When Toyota first purchased machine tools to make cars, it had to import these from the USA and Germany. The long distances involved meant that it was hard to get spares, contact the suppliers or even read the instruction manuals.

Toyota learnt all about the machines by having to disassemble and reassemble them. It also learned what it liked about the machines, where the weak points were and which functions were essential and non-essential to the successful exploitation of the machine tool.

Companies like Toyota now build their own machines, minus bells and whistles, for the specific purpose they want. These machines are generally 'right sized' to avoid the all-singing and dancing monoliths that become such a physical barrier to flow and kaizen. They know how to maintain these machines, can fit standardised parts, so that the spares profiling is a simpler and cheaper game, can standardise machine tools across plants, and do all of this at a fraction of the market cost. Toyota does not make all of its own machines but stays extremely close to the vendor for those that are purchased.

Not many businesses can afford to make their own machines or have the clout to influence machine tool vendors strongly; in which case, automation and error-proofing devices had best be simple. Engineers would do well to remember that capital Pounds, Dollars, Rupees and Yuan are scarce, but thinking is free.

Yet we risk being caught on the horns of competing requirements; the increasing need to error-proof our processes, but not overburden them with complexity. Our ideal outcome is a simple, zero-maintenance, easy to troubleshoot device that solves the problem at hand whilst retaining the flexibility to respond to changes. Changes that require us to rearrange, simplify, combine and eliminate steps in a build process countless times over the life of the product to stay competitive.

Traditional error-proofing control systems are inflexible to change and not conducive to kaizen or frequent product changes. They often rely on the technical knowledge of one or a small group of individuals. We have to find a better, more flexible way. A karakuri way.

2.5 Key 5 - One or many: The sourcing conundrum

Purchasing for critical parts is another part of this thorny equation. It should be a joint effort between purchasing and engineering to avoid the temptation of supplier selection based overwhelmingly on the lowest landed cost; the worst of one-dimensional approaches.

Several years ago I had a discussion with a Toyota veteran, at that time working in Delphi, who expressed dismay at Delphi's supplier roster of 4,500 companies (a result of its vigorously self-defeating pursuit of the best price for each discrete component). In stark contrast, Toyota would have aimed for a 250 strong supply base to avoid baking fixed cost into many places. In his view, the unappetising result of a huge supplier roster was limited contact with each supplier and complications during new product introduction (including ramp-up and ramp-down) especially where there are three or four suppliers for the same parts.

The Toyota approach was to spend time with good suppliers and work with them to reduce costs. Of course, we have to avoid placing all of our eggs into one basket and mitigate supply risk, but must not use these as an excuse for supplier proliferation. Remember the earlier comments about suppliers moving up the food chain to become systems suppliers. We make decisions to climb into bed with certain suppliers in long-term partnerships. The cost of an ill-considered one-night stand can be tremendous. The skill lies in selecting a compatible bedfellow.

The Boeing 787 Dreamliner makes for a compelling case study on the perils of a risky sourcing strategy. Boeing designed the plane, Boeing assembles it and markets it, but it is manufactured by 40 or so different international partners. This is a global supply chain for a plane that is sold out until 2015 – and is made of 50% carbon composite to cut weight and thus fuel emissions by 20%.

Unfortunately, this particular sword is very much double-edged. Three years ago the Dreamliner sourcing strategy was touted as the breakthrough case study for global collaboration. Now it is largely seen as a cautionary tale. Not that the strategy was "wrong" but, as one Boeing insider put it in an LA Times interview in Feb 2011, "there were too many firsts all at once". The Dreamliner currently sits in the parlous position of being 3 years late and billions of dollars over budget. Core competence engineering/design was outsourced to an enormous supply base that needed extensive hand holding. Boeing, sadly, did not have enough hands to extend in support...

On a broader point, consider environmental issues such as emissions and the focus on global warming and sustainable energy sources. Global supply chains will have to become a lot smarter and slicker to reduce carbon footprints and wastage. Consider the sheer volume of cardboard, used to deliver parts, which you still see in and around most factories. All of this goes to landfill.

Reduction of waste - leaning the supply chain - can be achieved many ways. One is to improve information flows to take us ever closer to the true end customer demand, avoiding the bullwhip effect of demand amplification. Similarly, using returnable packaging loops with RFID cuts out, at a cost, a whole world of pain that our logistics colleagues feel only too acutely. Toyota's final assembly plant in Burnaston became the first UK automotive car maker to achieve zero landfill several years ago, a target that is decreasingly aspirational and increasingly expected.

Overseas sourcing can only ever be a part of the solution, assuming that we truly understand the total cost of acquisition. Previously we mentioned the 'source globally, assemble close to market' strategy, driving even our mightiest manufacturers to maintain a manufacturing/assembly capability in Western Europe. There are a great many small to medium-sized businesses that struggle to generate the economies of scale to justify sourcing in low-cost economies.

As a nation, we cannot outsource everything overseas; for practical as well as economic reasons. Someone in the country has to make something to maintain the equilibrium of a balanced economy. The sobering fact is that 3.5% of our adult UK population, more than 1 million people, currently work in call centres.

2.6 Key 6 - Education, Education, Education

So, how does manufacturing at home look? There are problems. In the UK currently there are seven million adults who cannot read to an adult level, 11 million of us cannot add up two three-figure numbers. Access to skilled and willing labour is becoming problematic.

This skills gap reflects an economy where a career in manufacturing is seen by many youngsters as deeply undesirable, one step away from working in the pit. Why work in noise, heat and oil when the service economy offers a far cleaner alternative? Companies like JCB are committed to retaining a manufacturing base in the UK and are working extremely hard to engage schools, colleges and universities. It aims to excite young students and entice them into engineering. Let us hope it and others succeed.

In the meantime, the EU is coming to our rescue to fill relatively low-paid jobs. Pre-recession, The Midlands was not short of vacancies for assemblers at £6 per hour and welders at £9 per hour. The gap was, in no small way, filled with contract labour from the former Eastern Bloc.

Thanks to the enlarged EU, young male and female Poles, Slovaks and Slovenians – to name but a few – came to England for varying periods to earn money. There is uncertainty as to how long these young workers will stay in the UK. There are questions about the amount of money that is being earned and sent back to home countries.

The fact is that we are in the EU and are benefiting significantly from this migrant workforce. The general experience reported thus far is of people with an extremely good work ethic and a high level of skill. As a manufacturing employer, why would you turn away skilled workers for vacancies that you cannot fill domestically?

In summary, many jobs cannot be easily filled. When they are filled locally there are basic problems with literacy and numeracy. When they are filled from the enlarged EU, a large proportion of people speak English as a second or third language. Think of the challenges in a manufacturing business where machines can be dangerous, tolerances are tight and time is short.

Standardised work written in English had better have some clear photographs! We either have to accelerate people up learning curves very quickly – which requires a level of training that frankly few are prepared to fund, especially for a contractor who may decide to leave tomorrow – or to make it easy to develop competence very quickly.

This means simplifying our communications and information flows to achieve quality and quantity targets safely. In a nutshell, the production and engineering management challenge now and into the future is to take complex problems and make them simple for the shop floor. In short, make it easy to do the right thing.

2.7 In conclusion

The world will continue to change and present us with stark choices. Let us hope we have the serenity to accept the things we cannot change, courage to change the things we can and the wisdom to know the difference. Environmental concerns will shadow our every move. We have to learn how to retain good people and accept that people often choose to move job frequently.

Labour will continue to migrate, and one member of the BRIC economic growth quartet - Russia - will have to find a solution to a demographic time bomb that means they are running out of young people. The country is depopulating at a rate never before seen in a developed nation enjoying an extended period of peacetime. By 2050 Russia is estimated to have shed 26 million people. High mortality and weak fertility rates combine to create the perfect conditions for depopulation. The reasons are not entirely explained by the known facts; a high incidence of cardiovascular disease, soaring murder rate and a pasting at the hands of the AIDS pandemic.

The Russian government knows full well that their economic future depends on having the hands and brains in place to drive it. Witness the desperate measures launched to control alcohol consumption or encourage the birth rate. The success of "Conception Day" where couples are rewarded with TVs, fridges or cash if they bear a child on a certain day of the year, is unclear. Brazil and China, too, will at some point face a shortage of young people to work if they continue to dip below the "replacement rate" (the fertility rate required for a population to keep replacing itself).

The equally challenging flipside of this demographic coin sees developed nations scratching their heads to find ways to pay for the spiralling healthcare and pension costs of aging populations.

Those businesses that survive can still prosper so long as they fully embrace the mantra that necessity is the mother of invention. Doing more of what you currently do just will not work. Those that are excellent have generally become so through need and crisis, not choice. If you work in a business that is not moving forwards, you are moving backwards and, if complacency is your problem, create a crisis.

Throughout the next chapter I'll pursue this crisis theme to explore specific and practical ways to survive in the lean, mean world.

Chapter 3

The Lean Business - Practical ways to deal with a crisis

"Which will prevail, the rabbit or the fox?"

3.1 What kind of fool would create a crisis?

The answer is, ironically, the kind of enlightened fool who isn't already suffering from one. Cast your mind back several years when, in general terms, the economy was growing, input costs were lower and the outlook was rosy. The concern at that point – at least for me trying to engage 18 MDs in a $4 billion business – was how to get people interested in improving their business. If margins are holding and new and existing markets are growing, why change anything? My concern was the lack of a tangible crisis to drive the business to improve.

The enlightened approach is to create a crisis in a macro sense in the same way as we would in a micro sense for a production line with a history of running very smoothly, with good quality, productivity and few stoppages. We take out a person to stress the line to **focus** local supervisors and engineers on uncovering and eliminating more muda (meaning waste, as in the classic seven wastes).

Racking my brain to list upsides to a recession is a tricky business. One of the few is elegantly described in the old Chinese fable about a Zen master and a student out for a walk one day. The master points out a fox chasing a rabbit.

'According to the ancient tale, the rabbit will get away from the fox,' the master said.
'I disagree,' said the student. 'The fox is faster.'
'But the rabbit will evade him,' insisted the master.
'How can you be so sure?' asks the student.
'Because the fox is running for his dinner and the rabbit is running for his life,' came the answer.

In essence, if you are running for your life, you tend to post a pretty good qualifying time. There is a strong chance that a team fighting a common crisis will outperform a team that is not (strong leadership is something of a pre-requisite here). The tough challenge is to view a crisis as a good thing to spark change for the better. However we phrase it – backs against the wall, backs against the water, when the going gets tough the tough get going – there is an opportunity.

The key word highlighted above is **focus**. When we find a way to focus our people on the right problems, they are capable of great things. The management task is, in no small part, to ensure that the right things are being tackled. Of course, today we do not need to create tough times, as they are upon us. Unfortunately, there are no silver bullets to cure business ailments. Even today, though, I see major businesses missing many of the basics.

What follows are some thoughts for weathering the storm and coming through the other side as a fitter business. It is important to remember that there will be an 'other side'; sunshine follows rain as surely as rain follows sunshine, and you will likely emerge, blinking into the sunshine, stronger in many ways.

3.2 Anyone can look...few can see

In other words, engage your people in identifying and solving the problems that are causing you and your customers the most pain. If times are tough, make sure your people know that NOW is the time to focus. Be transparent and specific about the challenges, whilst treading the fine line between ensuring that concerns are commonly shared spurring a need to act, and avoiding scaring your talent away into the warm embrace of the competition.

Nature abhors a vacuum and rumours are rarely better news than the truth. Good times or tough, everyone should think about cost every day throughout all levels of the business. Engaging your people in the fight is the central point of this chapter. If the rabbit does not know that the fox is chasing him, he may lope along in blissful ignorance.

In the last 10 years, I have been asked too many times (the reason for the phrase 'too many' will become clear below) by the Managing Directors of manufacturing businesses to help urgently improve a poorly performing line. After clarifying 'poorly performing', I did a similar thing each time. Having introduced myself to the team leader and asked a few questions, I would stand on the shopfloor and watch the process for as long as I needed to gain some understanding, typically half an hour. This yielded clear areas to focus on and I would walk over and, with the team leader's permission, ask his or her associates some questions and get suggestions.

Typically, I would take this back to the MD who would be mightily pleased and call the managers to get started. It was at this point that I would declare that I did nothing but speak to the team leader, watch the line and ask the associates about their pain; and that these are things that the MD should be doing, and coaching the managers to do, without needing to call a Lean Queen like me. By the way, in one case the line was right outside the MD's office window, maybe 5 yards away.

In a similar vein, I was once flown to Belgium and then Peru to troubleshoot a windscreen-cracking problem. This one was solved for me by the setter in Belgium and the team leader in Peru. All I had to do was encourage them by asking the right questions. The footnote is that, almost always, the suggestions had been made before, but ignored or lost in the noise of running an operation. In tough times, pin your ears back and open your eyes.

3.3 Deckchairs on the Titanic

I am not saying wander out anywhere into your business and watch anything: that would be pointless. I am saying that once you know where your business is haemorrhaging, it helps. If you have no form of policy deployment – Hoshin Kanri – now is the time to get cracking. If your employees' goals for the year are not aligned to their supervisors', which are not aligned to their managers', which are not aligned to the business strategy, you are whistling into the wind. The policy deployment of the business should be driven by the vital few things that will improve the business. So what are your business issues?

Poor ROI?
Lead-time too long?
Poor quality?
Prices too high?
Capacity bottlenecks?

Where are you hurting existing customers? Assuming that these are customers you want to keep, your attention should turn here quickly to ask "How am I making it easy for them to source away from my business?" Is it due to late delivery? high defect rates? or unresponsive lead-time?

As an important sidebar, assuming that you are taking a look at your business whilst asking where you can improve to protect earnings and survive, be very careful not to use your improvement or lean programme as a guise to find ways to reduce headcount or labour cost by sending people through the door. If there are tough decisions to be made quickly because of a sharp downturn, and you have no choice, make it transparently obvious that the improvement programme is how the survivors will help get the business fitter to avoid the same in the future. (The advice of Machiavelli to the rulers of Florence holds true today: give bad news all in one hit and drip feed good news.)

If you send a worker through the door as a result of an improvement activity, listen for the tumbleweeds as you ask for kaizen ideas next time round. People are not fools and turkeys do not vote for Christmas. Hopefully, if your business is seasonal, you are able to maintain a ratio of temps to perms so that the core workforce is protected and temps come into the business 'eyes wide open' as to the personal risks.

Now to the cost profile within the business. The following is not definitive and there are things in here you may not agree with. They are my initial thoughts and a starter for ten. Take what you like and leave the rest.

3.4 Dealing with Material & Labour cost pain

Of the major cost drivers, *material, labour* and *overhead*, if your major driver is material cost, consider questions such as:

(i) How well are you procuring material at best price?

(ii) Are you making the most of your negotiating power?

(iii) Is your make/buy in good shape?

Take a cold, hard look at the make/buy if you are vertically integrated throughout the factory – for example, you buy and cut/bend pipe for fuel systems and are breaking your back making simple commodities at uneconomic margins. Remember, though, that outsourcing has an effect on contribution.

(iv) How well are your material planners bringing material in only when required, not before?

This is a question that will often point you back to noise in the production planning, information flow problems and production issues that force frequent replanning.

(v) Have your planners got used to running with too much fat in goods inwards stock?

(vi) How quickly are you getting material through the business?

Remember, reducing the timeline is the goal. How far can you drive towards the holy grail of 'being paid by customers before you pay suppliers' by having the absolute minimum inventory – and therefore lead-time – to keep the system working? A rough-cut value steam map for major product families – those with a large percentage of your turnover and/or profit that are hurting you in some way – will show you unconnected process islands within the factory with quick opportunities to take inventory cost out of the business via simple FIFO or pull signals.

(vii) How smart are you in ensuring that incoming deliveries are optimised?

I lose count of the number of times I have sat with materials managers to create, in Excel, a list of bought-out part numbers with the cost per unit multiplied by the current inventory to give, in descending order, the basic cost of the stock we are holding. So far, so obvious. The next step is to add two columns on the end for supplier location and frequency of in-bound delivery. You would be staggered at the number of times I find that several suppliers of fairly high-cost items have been delivering monthly when they are located less than an hour from the factory. Sometimes they are sacred cows; most often the question has just not been asked.

Consider the seven questions above before traversing the more challenging terrain of consignment stocking, VMI or establishing waterspider style collection services. To be clear, I am not advocating screwing suppliers as costs forced down the supply chain are still *within* the supply chain and often return in disguise.

(viii) Can you help your suppliers by improving your information flow to them, communicating changes quickly to reduce the interface waste of large inventory loops?

(ix) How well are you using your material?

That is, calculate the yield of high cost materials shown as a Pareto of scrap types by quantity and cost. Then go out with your engineers into the factory alongside the supervisors and get some basic, quick, problem-solving done. Make scrap bins smaller and transparent, and take them out from underneath benches. You want everyone to see this stuff and appreciate how fast scrap is being produced. I understand that this is all basic stuff, but it is not being effectively done.

(x) A look at the stock losses by part number by value – and/or overs and unders from stocktakes if you do not run PI (Perpetual Inventory) – will show you possible Bill of Materials (BOM) errors. There is nothing less sexy than a BOM error, but they drive a huge amount of waste.

A cross-docking operation, or indeed any that involves large and frequent movements of parts in and out, will find many opportunities to improve. Observing the unloading, booking-in and subsequent storage of the load from a supplier truck provides an eye-popping experience. The wastes involved in tackling incorrect boxes, poor or missing labelling, unplanned decanting, wrong and damaged dunnage, mixed pallets, mixed boxes, incorrect paperwork and segregation of diverted parts multiply like rabbits due to the sheer number of individual boxes / pallets that are moved around. A proportion of these wastes will be caused by your suppliers (and possibly your inability to be clear about supply requirements). In compensating for these shortfalls in supply requirement, week after week, you are effectively paying twice.

If labour cost is the significant driver, the questions are different but no less simple. Productivity improvement has never been short of column inches so I'll keep this brisk:

(i) Where is the labour density within the factory?

(ii) Do you have two lines side by side, the first requiring 5.3 associates and the second 6.3 by calculation; yet you man up with 13 across the two? Are you allowing that 0.7 opportunity to slip away through lazy balancing or a lack of thinking creatively? Even 0.1 of a person is still one person.

(iii) Similarly, do you have machine minders to man-mark each machine? Are you using the operator waiting time while a machine is cycling?

(iv) Have you standardised, or at least sized, line feeding work and ensured that fork lifts do not often ride around the warehouse and factory with empty forks?

This is where a deeper understanding of standardised work pays dividends. Type I - repetitive short cycle time work - is fairly simple to standardise but most people stop here. Type III - long cycle, indirect work like line-feeding or changeover - is harder but yields as much productivity benefit. Also, standardise the regular planned downtime elements of the day like start-up, 5s or TPM time. Start-up is a key time as a minute lost here is multiplied across many people. If you're smart, you consider ways to use short periods of unplanned downtime to complete non-value added tasks (and possibly free up time later top catch back from the stoppage) possibly via a kamishibai t-card approach.

If lateness because of capacity bottleneck is a problem, the constraint management regime – identify, elevate etc - is simple and well documented.

If overhead cost is a significant driver, then focus here. Likely you will have opportunities on all three fronts. The point is that you probably do not have the resources to fight all problems on all fronts. This leads us back to policy deployment and identifying the 'vital few'. Ingrain the Pareto principle into all of your people and ensure that you help them use the 80:20 outputs to create specific, aligned objectives.

3.5 Fight the fight at the right enemy

Weigh up opportunities against ease, cost and impact. If the impact is large, the cost-to-do small and it can be done quickly, then do it now. You will have gathered that the age-old entreaty of genchi genbutsu – go, look, see – is common to all of this. A tough question, which should be simpler to answer than it actually is in many businesses, is, where *exactly, specifically, precisely* is the business hurting? What are the cost drivers? What specifically are your losses on the factory floor?

It took me several jobs to realise the importance of an on-the-ball Finance Manager/Management Accountant. In times like these, they should be the ones holding everyone's feet to the fire and asking tough questions around cost make-up, productivity, good use of small capacity increments and contribution.

A good finance function is key to driving the business forward. If they are just reporting numbers in history, then they are no more use than a mortician at a post mortem, rather than the health advisor/doctor they should be. Is your finance manager saying: 'stop smoking and cut out the pies' or 'pass the scalpel'?

Don't forget other support functions. Is Manufacturing Engineering earning its corn or do you see the engineers mostly sitting at their desks? Have they squeezed every ounce of capacity out of existing capital before asking to invest in more? Are you focusing manufacturing on the quality and productivity losses that *they* can affect?

Is the maintenance function doing the right preventative work in the right areas and are there clear ownerships and hand-offs with manufacturing? Is HR earning its keep in terms of supporting the value-adding parts of the business to manage their people – recruitment, talent identification, retention, counselling, disciplinary, absence management? If you have in-house trainers, are they training things that are aligned to the business needs?

How do we practically get everyone to think about cost every day? Why not task someone in the office to monitor and reduce A4 and A3 paper usage. Ask whether everyone needs a printer or if some can share, question the amount of colour printing, ensure that everyone sets their printing default to duplex double-sided printing. If consumable items are a cost driver in the factory, give two different team leaders responsibility for reducing the consumption of gloves and safety glasses respectively: some people appear to eat these items!

If we truly believe that many small kaizens make a difference, we should be setting these bite-sized tasks. Walk around the factory in the dead of night and listen for the eerie hiss of compressed air leaks. Look at the cost of oil consumed by refilling leaking machines. I understand that all of this is basic, but ask yourself whether you are missing any tricks.

Above all, do not settle for mediocrity.

There is a school of thought that says you do not have to be the fastest gazelle to avoid the big cat on the savannah: just avoid being the slowest. This is a dangerous, dangerous game of doing just enough to survive.

Chapter 4

The Lean Business - Is this a walk through a great factory?

"Lipstick on a pig"

4.1 A virtual walk through a lean factory

Enough talk, let's walk...through a "Lean" Factory.

My last boss had the advantage of being both knowledgeable and entertaining. Not unicycle-and-bucket-of-glitter-entertaining, but he was a storyteller. I knew when he had an important point to get across as he would start a story and, sure enough, I would pin back my ears and try to pick the bones out of what he was saying. Take fork lift trucks, for example.

We had been in one of our factories the previous day and were talking about it.

'I didn't sleep so well last night,' he said.
Politeness dictated my response: 'Oh, why?'
'I had a nightmare,' he volunteered.

He proceeded to tell me, without smiling, that his biggest nightmare was being hit by a fork lift truck in one of our factories.
He then added: 'Do you know what my second biggest nightmare is?'

'That its forks will be empty when it hits me,' he said, without the hint of a smile.

These two sentences were all I needed in terms of direction. We needed to improve the safety of the fork lift truck (FLT) driving urgently, then improve their drop-offs and pick-ups – think Eddie Stobart – in the short term and work towards getting them off the factory floor altogether in the long term, with right sized packaging, delivery quantities, etc.
I remember this conversation clearly and will probably never forget it, as

he understood intuitively that people respond to and learn well from stories. In this same spirit, what follows in this chapter is a story, at the heart of which is a deceptively simple question - Is this a walk through a great factory?

Imagine a walk through a factory that had worked hard to use and sustain lean manufacturing principles. Imagine it had linked these separate tools to go beyond process improvement to flow improvement and on to system improvement. Strip away the posters and slogans and the fakery of following the 'royal route' and venture off-road into the cells and the warehouse.

What would you see in a really good factory? Does the presence of these things mean that it is a good factory? Is everything that glitters, gold? This story cannot be exhaustive or you would be holding a brick of a book right now. Equally, of course, what follows cannot be 100% correct as I can only talk in generalisations. These are things that are generally held to be best practice in the factory.

4.2 Brief encounter

Imagine that you have a friend who works for a business that is celebrated locally as a good place to work and is recognised in the community as a good factory. It has taken you many months of badgering to get a chance to walk it with the Manufacturing Director, Mick.

Today is the day. Mick greets you at the door and asks what you want to see.

You say: 'Everything.'
'What specifically have you come to look at?'
'Good practice,' you say.
'Good practice of what?' he presses.
'Everything,' you say.

Mick politely asks you to reschedule for the same time next week and come back when you know what you want. He gives you a warm shake of the hand and strides away.

The next week you turn up at the appointed hour clutching a list of specific items that you have thought about all week. Once again, Mick greets you and you start to reel off your list. He stops you after a couple with a hand on your elbow and says, 'Follow me.' Of course! Mick wants you to focus and get some benefit from the visit rather than blithely wander about ooohing and aaahing.

Mick is my kind of man. He avoids bland statements and management speak, talks passionately, and is honest about the struggles and current failures. You are not in for an easy ride as he challenges you on the way around and requests that you give him three good and three bad specific points at the end to exploit your fresh eyes. This is the quid pro quo. In hindsight, you realise that Mick made good use of his walk with you by using the time for his regular factory patrol as confirmation that processes are being followed and reacted to correctly. He acknowledges people, but does not disturb them unless necessary.

Some time ago Mick was struck by the words of Fuji Cho: 'Go see, ask why, show respect.' This is his aim. He walks you first to the shipping dock.

4.3 Shipping dock, Customer delivery & finished goods warehouse

'Why have we started here?' Mick asks you.

The answer he seeks is that it is closest to the customer and he likes to walk the value streams in reverse to see how each process is linked to its customer and pulls to their signal. You start at some kind of dry wipe shipping board showing the plan of outgoing trucks for today in clear delivery slots – you can see if they are ahead or behind. The plan reflects regular intervals and the minimum of dock doors are being used.

The dock workers have standardised work and their workload is levelled as far as possible by the way deliveries are planned. Mick leans into you and asks if you have noticed that everyone we have passed so far has had the correct PPE on and that gangways have been clear.

'Not always the case,' he volunteers.

He takes the chance to tell you that he had some help designing the factory layout so that all gangways were straight, avoided crossover of material flow and that there were no dead-end gangways.

'We like line of sight here,' he adds. 'You'll not find too much here that is taller than about a metre and a half.'

You spot a customer truck driver unloading empty returnable containers from his wagon and placing them in a marked lane. Like all stock/material areas in this factory, it is a calculated size to show when a problem occurs. Shortly, on a timed route, a tugger driver comes along, collects a stack of these and follows a route – like a bus – to deliver them back to the production cells. There are no sodden leaves to pull out or rainwater to drain away in these boxes. In 20 minutes, he will be back with a load of finished goods that he swapped for empties on the way round. Again, he drops this in a marked staging area ready for the next truck.

The dock supervisor knew these were coming. By the way, neither this tugger driver nor any of the others are on their phone whilst driving. His tugger is mercifully free of empty coffee cups and rubbish in the footwell and on the back. In fact, there are very few forklift trucks and they only operate on the docks. You rarely see a material handling device without a load of some kind. The small amounts of finished goods you see around you follow the same principles as all supermarkets in the factory: FIFO rotated, part number shown, min/max levels marked. Mick quizzes you on the difference between buffer and safety stock.

4.4 The Assembly area

As you walk into the main factory from the warehouse, you notice that the ceiling is not oppressively crowded with ducts and hard-wired service drops. The overhead lighting is good and working, better in areas where fine assembly and inspection work is expected. You approach the first assembly cell and walk inside it to get a better look. Mick rebukes you quickly and tells you not to interrupt their routine and muscle memory.

'Most defects and accidents happen when something changes', he adds.

He invites you to stand and watch this cell with him; the associates are unfazed because they know what he is doing. After a couple of minutes you become jittery but he stands there, stock still, not speaking for 15 minutes before wondering over to an associate to have a quick conversation that you cannot entirely hear. You hear the words 'stretching' and 'waste'. It seems good natured. He then goes to the supervisor area for a brief exchange.

The supervisor area is close to the cell and is home to materials and quality people, as well as supervisors. It has low walls and exceptional 5s that clearly states: 'Do as I do, not as I say.' You spot a colourful training matrix that shows current skill levels and targets to get more versatility.

'We aim for 3x3x3 flexibility mostly, but it depends on the number of people and complexity of the process,' Mick explains, as he turns off a fan that has been left on unnecessarily and visually scans the waste segregation bins for mixing.

'What did you notice during that 15 minutes?' asks Mick. You offer the following:

"The people here are wearing the correct PPE – you can tell because it is posted on the wall – and spend most of their time building products or operating machines; they are not walking to get materials or hunting for parts. Good parts and defects are clearly separated and marked. Defect bins are small, transparent and in a visible place to fill quickly and force a reaction.

If the operators have a problem they use the andon; in fact, I heard the andon tune more than I expected to. Interestingly, these andon tunes were turned off quite quickly, showing a quick response.

There is a clear production plan for the area showing production sequence and quantity. In this case, it is a heijunka box with a clock on top and slips of paper in small slots. The plan is visible to all operators, the setter – to prepare for the day's changeovers – and the line feeder. There is an hourly output chart showing specific reasons for gaps between plan and actual output.

Productivity is tracked for the days of the month and next to it is a follow-up sheet for kaizen ideas they are working on currently. The entries are recent and in different coloured pens and handwriting, actions are specific and the owner column never says 'all' or 'team', but is always a named person. There are dates and late actions have been highlighted for chasing.

There is an absence of big conveyors and equipment is close together, but still gives safe access and exit. On certain stations, benches are covered in protective material to avoid damage, but I noticed that it looks ragged in places. These benches are big enough only to do the work, with no spare shelves to accumulate parts/rubbish. Apart from the bench tops, there is a noticeable lack of flat surfaces".

Mick explains his seemingly trivial insistence on not putting things down in temporary homes (as it drives good 5s thinking) and shutting cupboard doors after they are opened to avoid trip and head-banging accidents. You wrap up with:

"Unusually, no parts are stacked on tables or floors. Subassembly quantities are controlled to avoid getting ahead. Parts are moving one piece at a time and seem to not stop moving. No one is sweating or waiting"

'Not bad,' says Mick, as he points out the team leader watching one of the stages to confirm that standardised work is being followed.

The team leader watches three cycles. You see him talk to the associate respectfully and they appear to be discussing the operation. You look at standardised work documents and see that they are written in simple language with few key points and reasons for each key point– if everything is a key point, nothing is – and some clear photos. The first two elements on this particular one are for visual neighbour checks on the previous operator's work. As he performs the check, the operator touches the areas of the part he is looking at and mutters something inaudibly to himself.

'We have half the number of quality inspectors we used to,' says Mick.

They have changed their job title and try to use these people to coach simple practical problem solving in the manufacturing teams as much as checking quality. He shows you a simple mechanical error-proofing device that was sketched by an associate to avoid a repeated quality issue they had with mis-assembly.

You notice that this assembly cell is right next to the machine that feeds it and that both areas are producing the same part number; they also change over at the same time. You have noticed that there are lots of visual signals in the factory; indicating at a glance 'on target', 'ahead' or 'behind', too much, too little, too high, too low, too hot, too cold. Having said this, the machines and areas have less paper up than in most factories. They have made an effort to avoid wallpapering. Red and blue tags, adorned by hand-written scrawl, can occasionally be glimpsed dangling from machines and jigs.

Mick sees you sketching in a notebook and tells you that visual control is at the centre of the training given to all supervisors. 'Our aim is that the supervisor should be able to quickly patrol their patch hourly and, without breaking step or asking a question, understand current status and therefore what he needs to worry about. Then they can get on top of abnormalities before they become problems', he adds striding on. Struggling to keep up, you once again notice, as he reaches a gangway regularly traversed by tuggers, that he looks right and left and utters a small word under his breath before crossing. This is clearly a habit.

4.5 In-house component manufacturing

As you pass into the component areas, you pass boards and posts with kanban cards accumulated and notice that, unlike your own factory, there are no kanban cards just lying around on top of benches or on the floor.

The production control people have helped manufacturing to establish buffer stocks and pull loops in only the right areas. It has taken a long time to get the understanding, but people now treat kanban cards like gold. You ask why there is an empty half disassembled rack lying on the floor.

Mick calls over the setter who walks you through a SMED improvement activity that he has done with the help of an associate and a manufacturing engineer on an injection moulding machine. The setter proudly declares that they have reduced changeover time on their most frequent and longest changeover from 37 to 14 minutes and spent £17 to achieve it.

The rack used to house parts that are no longer needed because they have halved the batch size and now changeover twice as often. Mick takes the opportunity to quiz the setter about the next steps. This section's goal for next year is to be making every part every day (EPED) to reduce inventory and lead-time. Mick has noticed that three red shirts are gathered around a press; red is the colour of shirt worn by maintenance fitters, so he knows there is a problem.

You notice a lack of paint on the floor to mark out 5s homes as tape is used, sparingly.

'We used to give absolutely everything a home,' explains Mick, 'but now we are much more brutal on what is essential in each area and try to design processes and tools better.'

The only reason for less tape is less stuff. He looks surprised as you explain that, in your factory, you also tape around the borders of 5 tonne machines; machines that don't move.

Your 5s discussion broadens to the fact that operators are obviously engaged in 5s. The checks and visual standards are clearly posted and they played a part in creating them. Mick shows you some one-point lessons for basic TPM on a machine.

'They do these every day to keep the machine healthy,' he explains. 'We've made them quick and simple, tried to eliminate hard to reach areas and marked oil gauges, etc. Of course, we don't ask them to do electrical testing or remove guards to replace parts, but we find that when the machine smells, sounds, moves or feels different, our operators are the first to notice.'

You notice that benches and the bases of machines are boxed off where possible – where it will not interfere with how the machine is run – to make 5s easier. In both the assembly and component areas, you witnessed nobody wandering away from their line or machine except for the break that started five minutes ago. The rest area was clean, well lit and a comfortable temperature. Water was available and the chairs and tables were in good condition. Three times on the trip through the factory Mick briefly picked up a part and visually checked it for workmanship. He explained that it was his chance, without speaking, to emphasise to his people how important quality was to him.

4.6 Material delivery & goods inwards

As you spend more time in this factory, the rhythm of material movement begins to strike you. All material movements are either kanban controlled, from or to a FIFO lane or one-piece flow. Mick tells you that the tugger drivers are like bus drivers, not taxi drivers, on a set route with a low cost for each customer journey, rather than the high cost of a taxi that drops you off and goes searching around empty for another expensive fare.

The tugger driver pulls up at, literally, a bus stop and delivers boxes of parts to well designed point of use racks, designed for associate benefit to deliver material to his fingertips.

In good Henry Ford style, the parts come to them at point of use, some in gravity fed racks and some on simple stands. Closer inspection of one reveals it to be fashioned from modular racking that can be altered; you would never know it, but this particular rack has had four different shapes over the years having really earned its corn. The backs and fronts of the racks have small photos or schematics with the part number that lives there to avoid misfeeds and mispicks.

You notice that the associates are not doing the Christmas morning unwrapping of parts so common in your own factory. The tugger driver, finishing his drop, pulls the kanban cards (taken from boxes consumed) from the nearby post and loads up the empties.

These empty cards will go back to the warehouse for the picker, if the route is decoupled, to pick the next load from the well-organised purchased parts market. The route you are witnessing is either fixed quantity/variable interval or variable quantity/fixed interval.
Some days he is whistling as he works, some days not. There is not much

cardboard about and your host proudly talks about their zero to landfill target. Mick goes into even more detail about the supermarket and bulk storage areas, the three different tugger routes – one for bulk items – the two-bin system that is in operation for heads and threads – outsourced to Heads 'n' Threads R Us – and the Plan For Every Part (PFEP) that underpins all of the material movement. He notices your glazed expression and smiles:

'It ain't sexy but it's got teeth,' he throws over his shoulder as you stride on to goods inwards. Mick does not amble around the factory; he walks at a specific pace for a specific reason.

You see an almost identical board to the one at the shipping dock. This one shows expected and actual deliveries for the week in timed slots against different doors. The board tries to level the workload of the dock doors and goods in workers, who also have standardised work. Mick comments that suppliers' ship a lot more frequently than they used to, as he tells you, with a rueful shake of the head, of the local supplier who used to ship once a month from a factory that was three miles away:

'I don't know how we missed that one...'

No extra shipping cost has been added as one of his people helped local suppliers form a milk round delivery/collection service.

This reminds you of something you noticed earlier. The proportion of the factory floor given over to stock is far lower than most other places you have seen. You see a driver unloading, under a canopy out of the rain, from a curtain-side trailer and putting the parts in a specific marked lane. One of these lanes is full and, Nathan, the supervisor explains that a tugger has broken down that morning and a supplier shipped parts early.

'Strictly speaking, we should have turned them away,' explains Mick, 'but this is a good supplier who has started delivering to timed slots this week and it's completely alien to them. We'll investigate and talk to them; Nathan thinks we might have contributed to the problem.'

Here the tour ends. Mick asks for your comments and three good and bad points. He lets you explain, listens, and asks questions to clarify and you notice that he does not jump in to defend or excuse. He asks you why you have not asked him whether they make money or not.

While talking to Mick you fix something firmly in your head. The next time you get the chance to look around a factory, you will not hurry through on a whistle-stop appreciation of shiny machines, smartly dressed associates and information-packed boards. You will loiter a while and feel the pulse, tune into the cadence, observe the cycles of activity. See, rather than look. The biscuits and tea back in the office can wait.

You tell Mick that this is the best run factory you have been to. He laughs and tells you that it is not possible for you to decide this based on what you have seen today.

'It is possible to put lipstick on a pig,' he adds. 'Come back next month and we'll look a bit harder.'

Mick, of course, doesn't exist. He is a composite character formed longingly in my imagination as the perfect lean advocate. In this chapter I wanted to convey both the nuances of his behaviours as he walks through his factory, and the practical nuts and bolts things that you would see in a truly lean factory. Sadly, a visual tour reveals only the external face of lean excellence. The next four chapters burrow deeper to illuminate some of the behaviours and cultural norms that underpin a sustainable lean culture.

Chapter 5

The Lean Business - 'Kodawari' means 'attention to detail'

"Snipers, cyclists and mechanics"

5.1 Tri, tri and tri again

I could make a valiant effort to cover all aspects of the art of being a lean business, but would fail on several fronts. Beyond the fact that I don't know them all, you'd end up having to cart this book around in a wheelbarrow. I choose, therefore, to be selective in covering the ones that are, in my opinion, either critical or have been underexplored elsewhere. I tend to favour the poor relation, the unfashionable idea that most people back away from as if it were a soiled tramp on a nightbus.

"Attention to detail" is one such area where businesses and their people must excel to survive. Where we have three words to describe the intricacies of "attention to detail", the Japanese have one: 'kodawari'. This chapter is packed with examples in an attempt to illuminate a nuanced subject.

A personal story to start our journey into kodawari. Earlier this year I competed in my first sprint triathlon – a 500m swim followed by a 20km cycle rounded off with a 5km run. As you embark on a flight of fancy that has you forming images of a bronzed Adonis; think again. I am a long way off feeling my ribs, or looking buff in a pair of blue speedos, but I do enjoy the challenge of sprint triathlon. To understand the kodawari in this case you'd need to run your eager finger down the list of results for the Cheshire triathlon 2011 to locate my name. A glance at my split times guarantees a furrowed brow as you struggle to compute the fact that my swim time was twice that of anyone else.

Kodawari, it turns out, matters in triathlon. My planning was very good; regular training, an improving diet, and shiny baubles of equipment that yielded arguable advantage but, oh how they shine. On the day of the triathlon I laid out my gear in the transition zones with the meticulous care of a fledging mother changing her first nappy, before joining the queue to begin the outdoor pool swim.

Perhaps it was nerves, perhaps my focus was distracted by trying to conceal the girth spilling over my swimming shorts from the gallery of family, friends and lovers surveying our every move, but either way I climbed into the salt-water pool and proceeded to grasp, with both brine encrusted hands, the dubious accolade of being the only one of 650 entrants who swam 1000m instead of 500m. This naturally screwed my time and I spent the first 6 miles on the bike cursing and berating my schoolboy error. It goes without saying that the error was all mine. Mea culpa.

How did this come to pass? Lean in close for a cautionary tale. My suspicion is that I half listened to the pre-swim brief and heard the steward state "16 LAPS of the pool (4 in each lane)". I then climbed in and did 4 LAPS in the first pool section before asking a Marshall, with vague elliptical hand movements, should I do "4 of each". Yes, she sagely replied. As it turns out I should have completed 16 lengths not the 16 laps (32 lengths) I did. 'Laps' and 'lengths' can mean the same thing to some people!

On the plus side I completed the affair without coughing up a lung and even managed the final 30 metres of the run arms aloft, semi-sprinting, wearing the same grim smile that I had previously employed in the closing moments of the New York marathon. Kodawari cost me 14 minutes – insufficient attention to detail.

5.2 Sky is the limit

Team Sky, the road cycling team, doesn't struggle in this respect. Team Sky wouldn't swim double the required distance. Team Sky is a serious outfit. I became convinced of this some months ago whilst digesting a newspaper article about their relentless drive to become the best cycling team in the world.

The Team Sky outfit have formulated a "winning strategy" with four core strands; trust, honesty, empowerment of athletes and (what the journalist in this case termed) meticulousness. Any or all of these strands could be equally applied to the lean environment and the requirements of a lean team. Our interest though is in meticulousness or kodawari by another name.

Reflecting upon the article, it was possible to trace all paths back to one overarching belief, and one man, Dave Brailsford, British Cycling's Performance Director and Team Sky Manager. Success via the "aggregation of marginal gains" is the name of his game and he has formed a fearsome reputation playing it his way. Essentially, it boils down to a belief that, at the highest levels of sporting endeavour, winning is rarely the result of being streets ahead in any one thing; the age of professionalism means that gaps of that magnitude simply don't exist now.

We succeed by being marginally better in many things – In the cycling example, the helmet is a fraction more streamlined, the frame fractionally lighter, the traditionally pocketed road shirt shunned in favour of a one-piece skin-suit, the diet slightly better - and it is the aggregation of these marginal gains that will put the Team Sky rider over the line first. No need to win by a mile when an inch is enough.

Brailsford himself offered a more elegant explanation of "performance by the aggregation of marginal gains" in a 2010 interview

"It means taking the 1% from everything you do; finding a 1% margin for improvement in everything you do. That's what we try to do from the mechanics upwards.

If a mechanic sticks a tyre on, and someone comes along and says it could be done better, it's not an insult - it's because we are always striving for improvement, for those 1% gains, in absolutely every single thing we do"

This section of the interview concluded with the comment "Naturally, all these tiny gains add up to a large gain".

So there you have it; kodawari and kaizen. Without consciously knowing it Dave Brailsford is a lean man. This chapter explores kodawari in three ways; an initial exploration of kodawari precedes a meander through some interesting examples (from the footwear of Colombian guerrillas to the performance of my favourite American humorist) rounded off with a serious look at how we apply kodawari for significant benefit in the 21st century lean business.

Kodawari is not consciously taught in Japan, neither has it been thrust upon the cream of Japanese manufacturers. It is largely inherent in the culture and represents the willingness to expend extra effort to understand and master fine details that will make your endeavour a success. As a simple example, a lack of kodawari in a CV or resume often precedes a hasty visit to the bin via poor spelling or inexplicably missing years between jobs. We interpret, fairly in most cases, the oversight of not spell-checking as a lack of care. A lack of care that we worry, as potential employers, may well be carried through to everyday working.

I do, however, want to avoid a largely dry academic discussion only occasionally enlivened by entertaining examples. The kodawari mindset deserves much more as its absence gives rise to serious yet insidious results. As a freelance lean consultant, many of the 'Groundhog Day' discussions I have surround the need to be specific in describing a defect experienced, or a waste seen, or the exact nature of a machine breakdown.

It is nearly impossible to countermeasure the root cause of a 'damaged' component because the word 'damaged' itself is such an all encompassing one. Adjectives like 'split', 'dented', 'scratched' or 'burred' are infinitely more useful than the bland uselessness of 'damaged'. The substitution of any of these words puts us a step or two closer to the root cause. Similarly, how do you countermeasure "machine broken" on a half a million pound machine with thousands of moving parts and reams of setting parameters. The phrase is simply too broad a church, too vague, a lazy description.

Perhaps this is why Taiichi Ohno favoured his chalk circle for Managers and Engineers to stand in. Forcing people to become attuned to the shopfloor, to see beyond merely looking. The point, I suspect, was not just to theatrically make a point, but to alter the way that the Manager thinks by forcing attention to detail in the place where value is truly created.

This is a particularly powerful approach for those who breezily declare that their patch has "no problems". The Japanese phrase is "Mondai nai" - literally – "no problem is problem". So stand in the circle until you learn to see the problems or even better, the abnormalities that will eventually flourish into problems. Kodawari in this sense means feeling the beat, flow, cadence, calibrating what is normal to be able to identify the abnormal.

5.3 Cyclists and cricketers

I'll open up with a few Dave Brailsford examples, a man deserving of a book all of his own, before covering more varied ground.

In the workshop where Team Sky bikes are stripped, tinkered with, conditioned and rebuilt they have taken pains to coat the floor in a colour that easily shows up a dropped nut or screw – a trick borrowed from motorsport. Why bother? Well, having applied kodawari to the design of the bike and stripped away superfluous parts – every part left has a job (and probably more than one) to play. Every part counts.

Brailsford's British cycling team flew back from the Beijing Olympics in 2008 with a fine medal haul (A total of 14 including 8 golds). During those Summer Games, the Brailsford approach to kodawari drove him to secure the BEST pit position in the Laoshan velodrome and establish rules for who was allowed access to the pit area during competition – only those racing and their immediate staff – to keep the cyclists focused.

Competing in a sport where milli-seconds separate finishing positions, Formula One racing teams have long fostered attention to detail in their engineering teams. During 2010, the McLaren F1 team were seriously investigating the way that logos are printed onto Engineers race suits to squeeze out another 100g of weight.

These are the Engineers, not even the drivers. Remember, though, that they now operate in a world where refuelling has been banned since 2010. Pitstops used to take around 8 seconds but have compressed to around 3 seconds; in races where overtaking is difficult at the best of times (even with KERS) and lengthy pitstops with the potential for cock-up have traditionally presented a chance to steal a place or two on the track.

Just ponder that time again. The car stops, has 4 tyres changed and is gone again in 3 seconds. Attention to detail matters greatly and a lighter suit can do no harm to the 17 engineers it takes to execute the delicately choreographed dance required to pull off a successful 3 second tyre change.

Take Cricket, and specifically the England team, by way of a final sporting example. For many it may lack excitement as a spectacle, but it offers up an enticing glimpse into the world of kodawari. Under the stewardship of Andy Flower, England have become world Twenty20 champions, regained and then retained the Ashes all in the space of 2 years...from a dismal starting point.

In a fascinating article dated August 2010, Simon Hughes of the Telegraph gave his "ten reasons why England will be world No 1". This fairly eclectic hit parade has kodawari, in different guises, very much at its heart. Here is Hughes, in his own words, on number 2 "Match Conditioning".

"The Loughborough indoor facility was also deliberately heated up to 30C to check on players who might be prone to cramp in hot conditions"

Later, on the subject of number 6 "Spit and Polish"

"It sounds basic, but many fast bowlers are so consumed by their bowling that they forget to polish the ball. England have developed a more strenuous routine centred around Paul Collingwood. They have also identified the men who have the least sweaty hands in hot conditions. The ball must be kept scrupulously dry to maximise reverse swing in such conditions so only these players handle the ball as it is relayed back to the bowler"

We are tossed another gem in number 7 "Field of Dreams"

"The fielding coach, Richard Halsall, has introduced a number of new tools for catching practice, including a special rubber ramp off which the ball, fired from a cut-down bowling machine, flies at unpredictable angles"

Flower is a man who, in Brailsford fashion, wants to win at a level where being very good is not enough because most other teams are already very good. Whether they would recognise it or not, I cannot tell, but both Brailsford and Flower are extending a lineage of deep analysis that stretches back through Billie Beane of the Oakland A baseball franchise and beyond. This type of focused data analysis establishes relationships between unexpected variables and forges counterintuitive cause and effect links to gain a small competitive advantage.

As a postscript, it turns out that Simon Hughes was correct in his prediction that England would achieve primacy in world cricket. In late August 2011, following a 4-0 whitewash of a once great Indian side, England snatched the top spot.

A change of pace now. In mid 2010 I drove to London in order to hear American humorist/author David Sedaris read from his books. He regaled an appreciative audience with some classics and took the chance to read stories from his soon-to-be-published book. In a satisfying application of PDCA and kodawari he was, throughout, surreptitiously adorning his script with a variety of marks to gauge the audience response. A belly laugh got a different marking to an appreciative ripple around the room. This informal but effective laughometer is, I assume, part of a process to refine his writing. That's commitment to an art.

A sideways leap takes us into the murky world of the military sniper; the kind of sniper who spends a good deal of his life prone and wriggling in the dirt. This sniper may have been tracking a target or setting up a shot for a long time and, here's the kodawari, exhaling at the wrong moment can ruin his shot. The knack is holding your breath as you lower your head to the rifle sight. If the sights are fogged up you simply can't take the shot.

To Colombia, and the year is 2002. Colombian politician and presidential candidate Ingrid Betancourt is captured by FARC, a guerrilla organisation, at a roadblock during an ill-advised road journey. She is subsequently imprisoned for over 6 years before being freed. What interests us is the preparatory training she had received to be able to distinguish between the army and rebels; not always a simple act in a chaotic country. She had been told that if the soldiers' boots are made of leather, you are gazing at the feet of an army soldier. Boots of rubber tend to belong to the unpredictable rebels and you should begin to worry now. This attention to detail matters and can buy time to decide how to respond.

Whilst I have no direct experience of warfare, I have several times been impressed by the attention to detail of soldiers operating in the theatre of war. It has become fairly common practice for soldiers to write their blood group (or attach a piece of sticky tape with it written on) onto the side of their standard issue desert boots. The reasoning behind this grim pragmatism needs no further explanation – an example of life or death.

Time to move on. As interesting as this collection of kodawari snippets are, we need to consider application within the Lean Business.

5.4 Kodawari and lean

Let's step inside the factory to look at tangible applications of the benefits of kodawari and the cost when it is absent. First, two contrasting occasions from personal experience. One where I didn't pay enough attention (detailed in the next few paragraphs) and one where I did (see the next section: "One hour and seventeen minutes").

It is June 2007 and by way of good-natured punishment for submitting my resignation to go freelance, I find myself dispatched to China to babysit a factory while the Operations Manager takes a holiday. This Shanghai based factory bore the hallmarks of most new facilities. The building structure, services and external landscaping had benefitted from deep thought. Step inside and the assembly track layout was OK, but the material presentation and flow was carnage. Large, jemmied-open wooden boxes lined the periphery of the track and parts regularly turned up in containers of all shapes and sizes - big ones, little ones, patterned or plain - including carrier bags. Like creating a beautiful body and forgetting to consider the blood that flows around it and sustains life.

Notwithstanding these issues, we decided that the line would be vastly improved via that well worn path to basic stability - a little 5s. So, we performed the usual hands-on 3s blitz activity and, at the finish, created a simple, visual, time achievable daily check sheet with the team members working the line.

By the way, I have rarely suffered from my inability to speak Mexican, Peruvian, Japanese, Indian or Chinese when it comes to working on the shopfloor - pointing and hand theatre often suffice. In fact, in Mexico I spent a week with 3 Mexican production line associates relaying out their cells. We got by admirably with the Mexican words for walk, load, unload, cycle time, machine cycle time, quality and maybe 1 or 2 others. I can still recall the phrases now.

Back to the main point. I had a gnawing feeling that I had been lazy somehow in this Shanghai 5s activity but couldn't locate the source of the itch to scratch it. The next day it came to me as one of the operators inadvertently pointed out an assembly problem as we were pulling apart the line balance. He had cuts on his wrist that were in the process of healing. I instinctively surveyed other hands nearby and saw that several of the men bore similar cuts on the wrists, some fresher than others.

This is when the penny finally dropped as I hurried over to one of those large jemmied-open crates I mentioned earlier. The nails were still protruding into the inside of the crate. As the operators were reaching in to gather parts, they were sustaining some nasty scratches. This was a factory where a reluctance to complain was probably borne of a desire not to lose an unusually good job within the area. In any case, it's wasn't solely their responsibility to point out problems. As discussed above, it was ours to look for them, to pay attention to detail and take away the aggravations of the job.

My laziness of thought - inattention to detail - had been to forget the purpose of 5s, the importance of safety, to not put the men of a manual assembly line at the centre of the improvement activity. I had forgotten to truly see. Maybe a chalk circle would have helped. Nothing was more important, at that point, in that factory than to stop another man getting scratched. This is 'respect for people' and I had forgotten it.

Art Smalley is not a household name. His fame stretches as far as the borders of leanland but not much beyond. In common with John Shook, he spent many years as one of the first foreign nationals to work for Toyota in Japan. In a manner of speaking, Smalley studied at the feet of the masters and now spends his time decoding the apparent black magic behind Toyota's success for the rest of us.

I don't recall the word kodawari in Smalley's articles or books but it is there, in the thinking nonetheless. Take the example of inventory reduction; more to the point, the need for it. The case for reducing inventory has been overwhelmingly and compellingly made for many years now, with beneficial impacts on working capital and the balance sheet. Whereas overproduction drives (and masks) the other mudas, structured inventory reduction (via a signal mechanism e.g kanban) acts as a means to safely stress the system and drive improvement.

It would be foolish to forget that excessive inventory was, and is, looked upon with fond glances by those who enjoy the comfort of 'a bit on the shelf' to allow for problems. Indeed, they might have won the argument if 'a bit on the shelf' hadn't proved so expensive and such an impediment to catching up with those deriving competitive advantage from reducing inventory.

The stalwarts remain, pointing to catastrophes like plant fires and tsunamis, to argue that we should have healthy levels of just-in case inventory sitting around...just-in case. This case has been systematically debunked by minds finer than mine; if 'just-in case' is your chosen tipple, the cup you choose to drink from has no bottom. Value stream thinking has taken us to the point where a critical mass of people are understanding the answer to the thorny question 'How much inventory should I have?'

The two answers, one technical and one philosophical (both right!) I regularly pedal are shamelessly adopted from Ohno, Shingo and others who trod the path long before me. Technically speaking the right amount of inventory is the minimum required to keep the system primed and functioning right now, to meet the first rule of not hurting our customers.

(second rule in my mind actually, the first being that everybody goes home with the same number of fingers, toes, and unimpaired vision that they turned up to work with). The attraction of this definition is that the answer is calculatable by looking at the stability of each process, the nature of batching process to process and imbalance in cycle times.

Yet, in isolation, there is a flaw to this answer as, if your process is weak, unbalanced, and riddled with waste, then reducing inventory to this 'right' or 'ideal' amount for the current state will only get you so far before you are overtaken by braver, leaner businesses. There has to be a future state 'right' amount to aim for. Hence, the more striking sibling of this twin definition, the philosophical one, argues that the right amount of inventory (assuming that you have satisfied the technical definition) is simply less than you counted last time. Nice and simple, but not what I wanted to talk about in relation to Kodawari.

Accepting the need to reduce inventory does not, of itself, reduce inventory. Value Stream Mapping, creating a future state, implementing pacemaker levelling, pull mechanisms and FIFO lanes help but do not tackle the risk of, inadvertently doing harm, by reducing inventory in the wrong areas (without tackling the problems responsible for the inventory in the first place).

The eagle eyed among you will be a step ahead of me, sighing, in the expectation of a lecture on the river of inventory, the boat, the rocks of problems and the need to reduce the water (inventory) level gradually to expose the rocks for tackling. Thus pull systems with a certain (arguable) level of stability behind them (and some levelling) provides a mechanism to do this. Stifle your sigh as I won't elaborate further, but will finally get to the point. The river of inventory is a great analogy but it falls just short in helping us grasp the right piece of string to start unravelling our inventory problems by understanding more about the rocks.

So we usher Art Smalley onto the stage with his clarity of thought and Kodawari. Not that there is anything new in this thinking. The problem, as ever, is that the clarity and attention to detail underpinning it has not caught on. Perhaps it's not quite 'silver bullet' enough for generations of leaders taught to look for the quick fix. The truth is, it requires a little thought in a world where thinking has lost its lustre. If you want to reduce inventory without jeopardising your customer, you need to stop thinking about inventory as one amorphous mass.

Smalley beautifully articulates the Toyota (and Honda, Nissan, HP etc) view that there are 3 types of inventory (or stock, to be lazy with my synonyms):

1) Cycle Stock - the level of stock you have to keep the process running. The amount you choose to keep lineside or between processes to keep the beast fed.

2) Buffer Stock - on top of 'cycle stock', buffer stock is extra inventory (often way downstream) that protects you against your customers' wildly varying ordering patterns. Most of us have worked with customers who appear clueless in terms of volume requirements, week to week (or day to day even).

3) Safety Stock - is the third level of stock that we layer on to protect us against ourselves and the inefficiencies within our manufacturing process.

It follows then, that one-size can't fit all in reducing inventory:

1) To tackle Cycle Stock we need to address cycle time imbalances within the process, reduce replenishment leadtimes by holding less lineside and waterspidering in some sense that suits our process. SMED earns its corn here. If you have to hold inventory, leadtime allowing, raw material is generally preferable to wip or finished goods.

2) To tackle Buffer Stock is often trickier. It generally calls for a look in the mirror to check that we are not distorting true demand patterns via batching rules. Quite often it leads to delicate offers to help our Customers improve or make clearer their scheduling. Greater visibility back into the Customer process can give us better information. We may even consider demand amplification across the tiers of the supply chain.

A decade ago, working in a first tier sequence supplier to an automotive OEM, the only way we managed to meet the p-time of vehicle launch to sequenced trackside delivery was to delve deep into the OEM's scheduling software and apply our own algorithms to what was happening earlier in their process - through body-in-white for example.

We may decide to absorb the variability, or a proportion of it, by having a finished goods buffer that fluctuates. Sure it's still inventory (the most costly type of all!) but it may buy time to keep the customer fed whilst we sort out the problems.

3) Safety Stock has us reaching for that mirror again to tackle our own Quality, Availability and Productivity issues.

The gift of Kodawari, thinking the way that Art thinks, is that it gives us a greater chance of success. I should also mention the work of Gwendolyn Galsworth in thinking more deeply about Visual Control and visuality. Her refusal to accept the usual vague exhortations to 'develop a visual factory' have generated a deeper understanding of exactly what will work, where.

One of the most encouraging applications of Lean thinking in the last 5 years has been the explosion of interest in Lean Healthcare. Surely there can be no more deserving application of expertise than to improve the way in which lives are saved and public health is improved, whilst using the tax we pay to best effect.

A strong example is the American surgeon Atul Gawande, who caught the eye with his pioneering work to make surgery safer both in the US and beyond. He developed a particular liking for the simple checklist to help surgical teams avoid the basic errors which can lead to surgical complications, including death.

Surgery, according to Gawande, whether in Mozambique or Minnesota, has four big killers - infection, bleeding, unsafe anaesthesia and 'the unexpected'. In simple terms he knew, from data, that problems caused by the first three could be significantly reduced with checklists to ensure compliance to standard procedures. It comes as no surprise that Gawande's attempts to introduce checklists to surgery hit some resistance.

A large number of surgeons consider surgery to be an art requiring, indisputably, a high degree of skill which cannot be condensed and diluted onto a piece of paper. The thinking continues that a master craftsman must be allowed to freely and flexibly apply his significant skills as the situation requires, without the straitjacketing of checklists.

This is the point at which Gawande learned how to sell. Success followed when he managed to convey the fact that he agreed and, in point of fact, checklists help remove the mundane (yet critical) burden of preparation and housekeeping items from the shoulders of the surgeon. Thus, the surgeon is freer to use their talent. Gawande knew that the checklists would work from the data he had collected on surgical complications (which had been caused by simple failures to follow procedure).

This Gawande preamble serves as a precursor to my real point - the nature of the checklist. In common with Smalley's approach to inventory reduction, it's not enough to decide to use a checklist. Deeper questions need to be asked about the purpose of each checklist. After experiencing some failures Gawande cast his net outside of healthcare to aerospace, amongst other sectors, to deepen his understanding.

He concluded that a checklist should fit on one page (to avoid the possibility of a second page becoming accidentally detached) with a mix of upper and lower case writing. A sans serif font makes reading easier. The words should be simple and exact and the lexicon should be that of the checklist user. He recommends between 5 and 9 items; a direct reflection of the belief that the human mind can juggle 7 plus or minus 2 items at any one time. If the time it takes to complete the checklist is any more than 90 seconds, Gawande starts to worry, as attention starts to drift and steps may be skipped.

Crucially we need to consider the purpose of the checklist itself. A DO:CONFIRM checklist will generate a very different outcome to a READ:DO. Either way, the 'pause point' as Gawande calls it (when the checklist should be used) has to be clear.

Be honest now, how many of you have thought so deeply about how to successfully use the deceptively simple checklist. Gawande has kodawari. In his mind, he has no choice, if he wants to save lives. His entire book (The Checklist Manifesto) is worth a read as he delves into a variety of other problems around successful interaction of surgical teams. The culture he seeks is very simple; to create a climate wherein a nurse feels comfortable enough to question a surgeon who has just skipped a step.

Gawande, Smalley and Galsworth have all scrutinised an area harder to truly understand and solve problems through the relentless application of, you guessed it, kodawari.

5.5 One hour and seventeen minutes

Allow me to share a recent kodawari success having earlier laid bare my 2007 failure. Fast forward four years to 2011 and I currently split my time consulting to four companies. The smallest is a fledgling MBO where every penny counts, revenue growth and cost control to survive are the main focus coupled with a need to stabilise Quality to generate repeat business. Somewhere, in other words, where a lean queen like me has to generate benefit - "wash their face" - quickly to justify their existence. On this day, I spent 1 hour and 17 minutes on the shopfloor and showed them where to save £50,000 per year starting today, at a cost of £12.

I have developed an interesting relationship with the MD of this business who is a good, smart man trying to develop a manufacturing business. Below is the summary email I sent to him that afternoon after I left the company. As a sidebar, even though we had a paid contract for my time, I gave this morning free to show him what he can find without needing to revert to me. I'd rather he used me for the more difficult work to get full value. I remain a fully paid up member of the "if a consultant has to solve the same problem twice, he has failed to transfer knowledge" school of thought.

From: russell@sempai.co.uk
To: MD
As promised, below is a bullet point summary of our discussion on the shopfloor earlier. The request was to spend today looking at Mould Shop quick-hit productivity savings to support labour cost reduction.

I observed the Mould Shop this morning between 8:30 and 10:00 - machines 3,4,6,7,10,12,13 were running. 6 operators in the shop, 3 perm & 3 temps. I focused on 4 machines primarily for the reasons given below:

Machines 3 & 4 - running LH & RH xxxxxx - **A quick look showed m/cs were being man-marked with a lot of idle time in between m/c cycles**

Machine 6 - running xxxxxx in clear material - **A lot of scrap outside and unidentified parts around the machine suggested a quality issue**

Machine 7 - running xxxxxx - **2 people were sat down for the first 30 mins I was there on what looked like a simple job with little/no fettling or flashing.**

I can only comment on what I saw today. Specific comments on the operation of these machines are below...**3 KEY GENERAL CONTROL POINTS** at the end.

In general I calculated your people to be working at 70-80% of sustainable "Operation Speed" i.e working rate over a full shift....so there is another 20% to go at, beyond this, in terms of "slow working" (more on this at the end).

SPECIFIC SUGGESTIONS

Machines 3/4 - semi auto operation, 1 person per machine. Each person had 21 secs of cyclical work (+ 2 secs non-cyclical making and labelling boxes every 34 parts) = 23 secs Operator CT per 58 sec m/c cycle. Mrs E and I set up a trial to run both machines with 1 person walking between them. Tom, your operator, tried for 1 hour at least and I timed him, after 45 mins, on a 30 sec CT per part = 2 per minute with very little waiting time (machine has to wait maybe a second or 2 for him). = getting almost exactly the same output with 1 person as with 2 = 1 man/shift saving * 2 shifts = £600+ per week.

At the moment, his boxes will need to be made up by your labourer but I calculate this to be 2 per hour = 16 per shift/per m/c = 32 per shift @ 1 minute each = 32 mins work per shift for labourer (or TL on afternoons). With some work on the bench size and orientation, I reckon your operator could do this as well. (I've assumed here that turning m/c around is a cost too far at the moment - the extra walk is the lesser of the 2 wastes). Need to write an SOP for this operation to standardise how it is done. To avoid leg-ache becoming a concern, rotate every 3/4 hours so max half a shift on this job; but as I say they are working at 80% "operation speed".

Machine 7 - should NEVER be a 2 man job - the only reason I can think of is if you are training someone new (foam has a knack to it) or there are quality issues (I saw some splash / finish problems) but Andy, in the cap, was keeping up fine. The m/c CT was 48secs for 2 parts and his work content was 17 secs per part = 34 secs for the pair. He has 14 secs per cycle spare - hence I can't see a need for 2 people at any point unless the splash / finish problems are really bad. Put some technician focus on the quality problem there and you could speed up to 40secs (that you run it at with 2 people) but with 1 person - he'd still have 6 sec per cycle spare and you'd get a 17% productivity boost.

Machine 6 - 1+1 tool - M/c CT was 46 secs for the pair and he had 25 secs of work content BUT lots of spare parts around. By 9ish he'd had 10 scrap out of 160 = 6% scrap rate for damage to only the one hand - looks to be after ejection by either (a) the one hand dropping on the other or it bouncing up and hitting the casting as it goes down the Mr F - made chute. Mr F has looked at this previously and we tried the net I nipped out and bought at Homebase BUT it needs to be tensioned more and slung higher to break the descent = more experiments. Persevere with this one as I calculate that this scrap is costing you £314 per 5k run per week =

6% of 5100 = 306 parts @ 31p = £95 per week

+ extra 4 hour run to run the matching hand (blanked off) to make up for the scrap = 4 hrs @ £35 per hour + £8 per hr labour cost = £172 per week

+ I think some of the "good" hand are going in the bin also = 50% = 153 @ 31p = £47

= total cost of £314 per week

It's worth Mr F pricing up a simple concertina chute (if the net idea doesn't work out) as the payback would be rapid.

I make this £1000+ a week saving for some quick hits

GENERAL SUGGESTIONS

I could include a lot here - 5s, Standardised Work etc but i'll keep it punchy. These are the MUST HAVES...by yesterday

Red defect bins at the end of every machine in a taped home - emptied end of every shift. Parts are either in the red bin or in the finished box...nowhere else is acceptable. Put the bins in the aisle so that all of you have to walk past them every time you go onto the shop.

You Mr G and Mr T each to pick a random part once a day from a red bin and ask the operator why it's in there to test their understanding of the quality standard and ensure that we are not being loose in throwing good parts away.

Every machine (including autos) to have hourly output boards at the same end as the red bins with target, actual, scrap and downtime (SEE ATTACHED). Train your operators to fill in their output every hour - good or bad. You'll need them to understand that it is to surface problems as well as establish a cadence. Blow-up the attached excel sheet to half-flipchart size and get it laminated (local reprographics company would do this for £20 ish). JUST doing 1. and 2. will get you a 5% improvement in output and quality.

Use your best setter to troubleshoot the flash/splash/short issues on your top 2 scrap cost parts (calculated from Mrs E's sheets). Don't do any more than the top 2 at a time.

As discussed earlier I'm happy to come back for the extra half a day once you have the defect bins, hourly output boards in place and the jobs on m/c 3 and 4 are running with 1 man. There's a lot more opportunity.

Thanks
Russell Watkins

Incidentally, in sharing this email my aim is not to blow my own trumpet but to show that anyone could identify such opportunities with sufficient kodawari. There is no sense of 'letting daylight in upon magic' here. The improvements were simple ones.

5.6 Control - and kodawari - before kaizen

We spend a lot of time discussing and extolling the virtues of kaizen and often forget that kaizen can only really successfully be built on 'control', to avoid shifting sands and the scenario where improvements cannot be sustained because of insufficient control/standardisation. Supervisor basic control of his area is, in my opinion, based on the holy trinity of Team Brief, Cell Patrol (walking the patch regularly to understand the current condition) and dealing with abnormality to return to a running condition as soon as possible.

During the last 3 years I have trained 60 Team and Group Leaders in a Toyota Group Company to perform thorough Cell Patrols to improve levels of control, based on the premise that most defects and accidents happen when something changes - either a planned or unplanned change. Planned changes are taken care of at the start of shift Team Brief. The other side of this particular coin is recognising when unplanned changes are happening...hence a thorough Cell Patrol is an essential skill for a supervisor. Kodawari makes the difference between a useful and useless patrol.

If you ask supervisors what they look for when they are walking their patch you're likely to tease out some general statements - "problems", or "defects". Dig a little deeper and you'll likely hear something more useful but incomplete "I keep an eye on the gauge on ABC machine" or "I look in the defect bin". These comments are a country mile away from the attention to detail required for a strong Cell Patrol; a patrol that does not require an aide memoire or checklist and that can be done without breaking step.

It is possible to teach this level of detail within five or so patrols but requires constant practice to enhance. The level of kodawari in monitoring defects is a good example. It's not enough to look at the defect bin to see if it's full. You are looking to see if all defects have been clearly separated from good material; whether the usual defects are present (a lack of the usual defects can be just as enlightening as it means that something in the process has changed and you'd do well to understand what); if unusual defects are present; if there are unusually high or low quantities of defects. Note that I set this paragraph up with the phrase "monitoring defects". By this stage it is already too late. The best control comes from understanding 'normal' and spotting 'abnormal conditions' quickly. This is truly the difference between 'good' and 'great' control. 'Good' control finds and deals well with defects. 'Great' control spots and resolves the abnormality before it has a chance to become a defect.

Similarly, looking for "safety issues" is too vague. The ability to identify and resolve safety problems starts with teaching people to keep a good 5s condition and look for specific problems; the most common and significant risks for the kind of area you work in. For example, I have trained supervisors in an HVAC factory to look for the correct PPE being worn correctly, overhead power drivers swinging around near the head, aisles being blocked, doors of cupboards left open, safety devices being overridden, fatigue matting wearing or broken, chemical cupboards unlocked, and items left in a temporary home to surprise somebody else.

Broadening our kodawari discussion, I have some simple indicators that I look for to gauge the interest and engagement of the management team in the shopfloor, its people and its activities. I'll walk slightly behind the Senior Manager to assess whether they are looking as they walk, how aware they are of forklift danger when crossing aisles, whether they cut corners, do they walk around while talking on their phone, are they respectful of not meandering into someone's work area and disrupting their movement flow; remembering that most defects and accidents happen when something changes. Do they understand that product changeovers and break-times (just before and just after) are some of the riskiest points in the day where a dip in concentration can flow a defect out to the Customer.

At another level again, we can assess the overall level of control on the shopfloor by confirming whether the various clocks dotted around the factory show the same time - often not. A strong team starts together and finishes together. Team Leaders around the world have the daily heartache of convincing their team not to pack up a few minutes early and queue at the clocking machine because the team across the gangway are allowed to (as their clock has been erroneously set 2 minutes faster).

If you want to gauge the level of control, be present at the start of the shift and at the end of the shift. For a bonus engagement question, look at how the rest areas are left after breaks; the comfort of the facilities are also a gauge of management respect for where wealth is truly created in the factory. You can tell a lot about 'respect for people' from the facilities they are asked to rest in. After 4 hours on your feet working to a 60 second TAKT Time you don't want to be sitting in a filthy area trying to keep the flies off your sandwich, and your sandwich off the cracked filthy table. Kodawari, kodawari, kodawari: From the MD all the way up to the on-line Associate, we all need it.

I could go into much more depth and dissect the attention to detail required to recognise and train fundamental skills, or write strong Standardised Work Instructions and train them well via the simple beauty of TWI Job Instruction. I could talk about the kan-kotsu (or knack) involved in picking up screws and feeding them dexterously through your fingers to present them easily in your finger tips; skills that can be taught to collapse learning curves and safeguard Safety, Quality and Productivity; but I won't, for fear of labouring the point.

Before we leave kodawari, one final comment. Fujio Cho, incumbent Chairman of Toyota Motor Corporation, once gave a brief summary of the philosophy behind TPS as he saw it. As long as I draw breath I doubt that I'll ever be able to match his succinctness; to say so much in merely six words. His exact words were "Go see, ask why, show respect".

At the base of lean, hidden to all but the most determined, is attention to detail. It may lay largely undiscovered because we naturally recoil from some of the seemingly obsessive behaviours that Japanese, and perhaps Toyota, veterans in particular have engrained into their behaviours. For example, the practice of walking in right angles around corners in factories to absolutely respect the gangway markings sounds odd, but understand the reason behind it and it makes good sense.

Perhaps the last word in kodawari should go to the men I mentioned earlier in this chapter - the snipers of the world. These men, having crawled painstakingly slowly using the sniper crawl (barely moving, no more than 4 inches at a time propelled only by fingers and toes) into range of the target, set about a process so disciplined that, ethics of the profession to one side, may well make snipers the poster boys for kodawari.

Imagine the sniper who, brandishing his meticulously maintained rifle, has to calculate his shot to compensate for humidity, temperature, barometric pressure, wind speed, wind direction, and for the fact that, if he has recently fired a shot, he has to allow for the heating that has affected the barrel of his rifle. If his shot is over 400 yards (let alone the official long distance killing record of more than a mile and half, held by a Canadian sniper operating in Afghanistan) he has to allow, mindbogglingly, for the Coriolis effect - the curvature of the earth. Having allowed for all these factors he then remembers not to exhale at the moment he pulls the trigger as detailed earlier. Oh, and during all of this he has kept his feet laid flat on the ground behind him so as to present as insignificant a target as possible to the enemy. This is kodawari.

Chapter 6

The Lean You - Flexibility

"The mighty oak or the flexible reed"

6.1 The sustainability key - lean leadership

Chapter 4 took us on a virtual tour around a lean factory in the company of Mick, the plant's Manufacturing Director. The chapter essentially asked the question: is this how a great business looks? Is lean limited to the visible, tangible application on the shopfloor of well-documented tools like 5S, SMED and kanban? The phrase 'Lipstick on a Pig' gave a hint to my belief that you cannot judge a good or lean business purely by what you see. Some pigs do wear lipstick.

What really counts is that which you cannot easily see. A number of years ago, I left a very good lean consultancy for two reasons. One was that my wife had borne our first child and I had been working solidly away from home. We made a simple lifestyle choice based on the fact that I did not want to be a father who came home, worn out, on a Friday night to a list of things my daughter had done for the first time.

The second reason was that I harboured a nagging fear that one day, in one training room, in one company; one operator would ask me the question I dreaded: 'How long do you spend in each business you help?' In this nightmare scenario, I would rattle off the structure of our kaizen workshop; pre-diagnostic, diagnostic, workshop and three one-day follow-ups for a grand total of 12 days over four months.

The next, simple question would be the killer blow: 'What can you teach us about sustaining these improvements?' Ah, the magic question. They could have phrased the question any number of ways: 'How do we go about making this a part of our daily business? How do I squeeze it all into my working day?'

I would have no good answer based on experience and did not fancy spending 10 years dodging the question. The kaizen workshop model was and is a strong model for what it delivers, with excellent consultants delivering it, but I felt ill equipped to answer the magic question. All I knew was that teaching people how to use kaizen tools like 5s, standardised work, data analysis and waste elimination was necessary but insufficient.

So I came back into industry eleven years ago to learn about sustainability. Those good people at the Shingo prize for Operational Excellence have been on to the need for more than tools for some years. They currently assess an organisation based on tools, systems and principles, not just tools. Useful judgement can only be reached by understanding how the organisation operates and is structured in relation to things such as:

- Product development
- New product introduction
- Supplier management
- HR management
- Human Resource Development (HRD)

All five of these are rich seams to be mined in response to Mick's invitation at the end of the 'Lipstick' tour to: 'Come back next month and we'll look a bit harder.' I'd like to focus on the trickiest of the five, in my opinion: human resource development. More specifically, the ability of the organisation to grow lean leaders who think and behave the right way and can coach others to do the same. Push me for a single word to summarise the contents of this chapter and I'd offer you 'flexibility'.

Before diving headlong into this chapter I should illustrate what the word 'flexibility' means to me. Several short stories follow, examples that I have experienced or spotted in books or the media, to explain this key lean leadership trait. The stories cover giant pandas, a stranded calf, a German retirement home and the averting of fights in baseball games; flexibility of thought knows no bounds to its usefulness.

First up, from our German cousins, a story that may well be my favourite by virtue of its simple elegance. A Dusseldorf retirement home was experiencing problems with Alzhiemers patients wandering beyond the grounds of the home only to be found lost in town. These were not isolated incidents and the sympathetic police developed a regular routine of rounding these straying patients and returning them to the home. The flexibility of the solution meant that, after its implementation, patients only ever wandered a few yards from the home.

How did they do it? The retirement home persuaded the local authority to install a bus stop outside of the home, genuine in every respect bar one. The sole anomaly being that no bus had ever, or would ever, stop there; a fake shelter. Patients would wander out, see the bus stop and start queueing. Periodically, staff would approach the orderly queue and gently break the news that the bus was not due until later, and would they like to come in for a coffee during the wait. Director of the home, Richard Neureither, completes the story for us with the fact that within 5 minutes they had forgotten they wanted to leave at all.

Meanwhile, 5000 miles to the east, Chinese conservationists at the breeding centre in Chengdu, Sichuan have been attempting to preserve Giant Pandas. They have experienced unprecedented success in rearing 300 captive-bred Pandas ready for release to swell the remaining 2000 existing in the wild. Much of the effort has been directed towards the difficult business of kick-starting their breeding habits.

Breeding Pandas is the zoological equivalent of knitting fog for a whole raft of reasons. In general the Panda is, ahem, notoriously 'inefficient' when it comes to the beautiful act of copulation to propagate the species. Generations of frustrated scientists, no pun intended, have stood by watching (more accurately not watching) and waiting for successful Panda mating. Reasons abound; the female Panda is only on heat for 72 hours a year and, during this tiny window of opportunity, can only fall pregnant during a specific 12-24 hour period. By unlucky coincidence, the male is not well endowed and pregnancy tends only to happen when a very exact position is adopted by both partners. As it happens, both partners tend to have poor knowledge of the correct position. To make matters worse, captivity tends to turn Giant Pandas off.

The unhappy icing on this particular cake is the fact that female Pandas, when they can be persuaded to at all, tend to bear 2 cubs and immediately abandon one to die as they rear the other.

In demonstrating resilience, kodawari and flexibility of thought, the scientists conjured up several pioneering techniques to boost numbers. Less successful ideas, including showing the Pandas videos of the correct position and slipping them viagra, culminated in aggressive and unfruitful exchanges. Some success came from creating the right environment for the bears by, for example, dressing scientists up in Panda costumes when in proximity to minimise human contact.

I can only second guess the thoughts wandering through the mind of a ridiculously well qualified scientist as she/he steps into a musty, slightly damp panda costume. Many years of intensive study and crippling personal debt prepared these hardy souls for this activity.

The greatest success for the project flowed from artificial insemination and subsequent close attention post birth to swap the two cubs in and out for nurturing by the mother. Thus she was tricked into thinking she was raising only one cub when in fact she was raising two. My wife is fond of airing the vaguely controversial opinion that their resistance to help, conscious or otherwise, is nature's way of telling us that the Panda's time is up.

Early in 2011, continuing the animal theme, Sky News ran a story about a calf which had become stranded on a frozen pond. The flexible thinking rescue helicopter pilot flew above the frightened calf and used the down-draught of the rotors to push the panicked animal to the edges of the pond. Even though the ice was broken by its flailing hooves, the calf was safely recovered.

Finally, a story from Japanese baseball. It is difficult to overstate the love that Japan has for the game of baseball, which enjoys a massive following throughout the islands. Thus, a well worn path has been beaten by fading American baseball stars to the Japanese Central and Pacific leagues. You'll appreciate that, with two very different cultures, as surely as night follows day, stories of cross-cultural misunderstanding will be legion.

Robert Whiting wrote a tremendous book on this topic called "You Gotta Have Wa". Wa refers to the Japanese team-centric sense of, and the word doesn't do it justice, 'harmony'. I'll let Whiting tell you, in his words, of one particular encounter where an interpreter showed great flexibility of mind. The 'brushback pitch' referred to below is a pitch thrown high and inside, usually a fastball, intended to force the batter away from the plate. It is not popular amongst batters. Whiting tells the story thus;

"Tony Solaita, an American-Samoan who played for the Nippon Ham Fighters, was up in arms over brushback pitches in a game against the

Lotte Orions and used his interpreter, Toshi Shimada, to raise the issue with the Orions catcher during pre-game practice the following day.

*'Listen you no-good son of a bitch,' said Solaita, who was built like a Brinks armored truck and had a temper to match, 'if you have a pitcher throw at my head again, I'll f*****g kill you'*

Shimada did not bat an eyelash as he translated: 'Mr. Solaita asks that you please not throw at his head anymore. It makes his wife and children worry.' The catcher flashed a look of appropriate concern. He bowed slightly, then assured them it was all an accident and promised that such a terrible thing would never happen again.

Solaita nodded. The two shook hands and the meeting ended"

Whiting concludes that Solaita, the batter, had defended his honour, the catcher felt some sympathy towards him and Shimada had the warm glow that envelops a man who has just averted a fight.

6.2 The silent flute

As I further pondered the question of coaching flexibility in lean leaders, a film I saw at least 20 years ago played at the edges of my mind. It was intriguingly entitled 'Circle of Iron' (aka 'The Silent Flute') and starred David Carradine as a blind, wandering sensei who tracks a young man (Cord) through a series of martial arts challenges to reach enlightenment. As a film it is plagued by a number of flaws: ropey acting, stilted dialogue and serious problems with the narrative thread. Fortunately, in a sea of mediocrity there are some standout moments.

The most notable comes to pass at the end of the film when Cord finally gets his trembling hands on the book of enlightenment, having overcome all obstacles in his way. When he opens the book, each page is nothing but a mirror and he laughs like a drain; apparently enlightened by this. This is my kind of ending, as it displays a truth that good coaches intuitively believe; that each of us already has, somewhere within our experiences, most of the resources required to tackle our problems and challenges. It is a case of finding them and learning how to access them when the need arises. But, I get ahead of myself.

Throughout the course of this chapter I'll simply replay five of the most useful conversations I have taken part in, each of which highlights a way of coaching lean leaders to think and act flexibly. My memory has been dredged to offer a transcript, as accurate as memory allows, of each; thus offering up a chance to explore the skill of a good lean coach. The conversations played out well in these cases. Inevitably, I could just as easily recount 50 other conversations where it ended in stalemate, confrontation or metaphorical tears.

These are not conversations you would have every hour of every day, simply because you would never get any work done. A good coach does not dispense gems of wisdom at every turn, but sees a relevant opportunity and grasps it. Selecting *when* is a skill all of its own. The scenarios below were opportunities taken by the coach when the wolves were not at the door, and there was a clear benefit to challenging the individual.

Bear in mind, also, that both parties in all of the scenarios already knew each other, so had a degree of rapport. Whilst the scenarios vary, there are clear common themes. Should the urge take you, I would recommend that you reflect on their approaches. Socrates would be a very proud man. Of course, there are no correct answers, but some responses are clearly more useful than others. I have the luxury of having been there to contextualise the conversations. A clue to the approach lies in the title of this chapter: 'The mighty oak or the flexible reed'.

You will find little to no comment on the nuts and bolts of the conversations that ensue as I have little to add to the subtle and elegant way these interactions were steered. Dissecting them would dilute the essence.

6.3 Scenario 1: Walk a while in another man's shoes

Why a lack of engagement fails

Jed – shown as J below – is a Team Leader looking particularly perturbed. He tells the coach – shown as C below – that he cannot get Markus who works on the assembly line to follow the standardised work when he builds an assembly. The standardised work has recently been introduced for the first time. Jed has been trying to persuade him for weeks, but Markus is really digging his heels in. 'I'm going to have to give him a verbal warning,' says Jed.

C: Standing by the line talking to Jed: 'Why do you want to give him a verbal warning?'
J: 'Because he won't follow it.'
C: 'Won't follow what?'
J: 'The standardised work instruction. He's being really awkward. Could you have a word?'
C: 'No, it's your responsibility to resolve this one. I'll help though. Apart from this problem, is he a good operator?'
J: 'He's been a good operator 'til now. Turns up every day, gets back from breaks on time, makes few defects and makes his numbers.'
C: 'Blimey, and you want to give him a warning. Which stage [of the line] is he working on?'
J: 'Stage 6 again today, but he alternates between 4 and 6.'
C: 'Which one won't he follow: 4 or 6, or both?'
J: 'Not sure. I only know about 6. Does it matter? He just needs sorting out.'
C: 'Why am I interested in whether it's only 6 or includes others?'
A few mumbled half-hearted answers, before a hopeful:
J: 'To know if he's got a problem with just that one or standard work in

general?'

The coach nods.

J: 'Hang on, I'll ask my setter when he was last on 4 and whether he had a problem then.'
C: 'Why not ask Markus? While you're at it, could you grab the standard work, please?'

Jed returns a few minutes later.

J: 'He says he's been fine without this bit of paper for three years so far and sees no need to change the way he does things now just because some office jockey comes and pins a bit of paper up by him.'
C: 'Who pinned it up?'
J: 'Me, but I briefed the team the morning that we put them out and I asked them to let me know what they thought.'
C: 'Was it printed in colour and laminated at that point?'
J: 'Yes.'
C: 'I'd be narked too. I'm guessing it was it the first time he'd seen it.' A nod. 'A laminated, typed, colour document doesn't indicate that you were very serious about asking his opinion. We'll come back to that. Does he feel the same way about stages 4 and 6?'
J: 'He's only really moaning about 6, and before you interrupt, I asked him why and he says his way is better.'
C: 'OK. What are you going to do now?'
J: 'I've tried explaining to him before that the standardised work shows the best way, it guarantees safety, quality and cycle time. I even explained that it helps with training, covering absence and it means we can move people about on the line without jeopardising things... all the textbook answers.'

C: 'What did he say?'

J: 'He said his way his better.'

C: 'I'm with him so far. Nothing you've said to him sells the idea of standard work. The real question has to be: what's in it for him?'

J: 'I've just told you that.'

C: 'No you didn't. You told me what's in it for you and our company. What's in it for him?'

J: 'Surely I haven't got to explain everything to everyone. It used to be that people did what they were told. We pay his wages, so he should just do it.'

C: 'Ok. Go and stand in the car park for me will you?'

J: 'Why?'

C: 'Because I want you to.'

J: 'Look, I see what you're trying to say now, but...'

C: 'No buts. I agree that you don't have to explain everything, but Markus spends eight hours a day here doing a repetitious job several hundred times. You come along and tell him to do it differently without asking his opinion beforehand and then give him no good reason. I'd say he's got fair reason to be moaning. Put it a different way, do you think that it's worth talking to someone if you want to change the way they spend half of their waking life?'

Jed nods.

C: 'Any argument has a logical side and an emotional side. Markus needs a good reason to change the way he has spent the last three years. If you gave him a warning now, sure he'd follow the rule while you were looking, but as soon as you go he'd revert to his own method… and you'll get nothing out of him beyond the bare minimum. How many people work for you?'

J: 'Fifty.'

C: 'You can't watch one man out of fifty all day, can you? You want him to follow it irrespective of whether you are watching or not. It can't just be a rule. Voluntarily following the standardised work has to be something people understand the purpose of and can believe in, believe it's the right thing to do, have a reason to do it, some benefit for them. What's in it for him?'

J: 'OK, OK... job security, long term.'

C: 'True, but that's a limited sell. Most people don't think that long term or make the direct connection that their own job influences the company's future. So, once again: what's in it for him?'

J: Thinks, grimacing: 'What should I say to him?'

C: 'What do you think you should say to him?'

J: 'I don't know.'

C: 'Is his way better?'

J: Sheepishly: 'I don't know.'

C: 'So, try both ways and let's see. Before you try that, how will you know whether it's better or not?'

They have a discussion about safety being the primary concern, followed by quality and then cycle time and ease of build. Jed then trials both methods with Markus.

C: 'How did it go'?

J: 'Both ways are safe; no problem on quality and the cycle time is almost identical. To be fair, both ways work. He's got a couple of good knacks, but he loses a bit of time as well.'

C: 'So, here's the real question. If he can meet the standard time, safely and make good quality parts, does it matter if he does it a different way?'

J: 'Of course. If people have a different way, we'd need to set the area up differently depending on who is working at that time. We can't have two or three different versions of the standardised work for one job. It's hard enough to keep it up to date as things are.'

C: 'Good… and that's just the start. Let's focus on just one thing here. Let's say Markus's line has a bad day and the defect rate is high, including a new type of defect you haven't seen before. You try to solve it and narrow it down to one part of the line. Is your job easier or harder when proven standardised work is in place and being followed?'

J: 'Easier because I can rule out some things.'

C: 'Like what?'

J: 'The standardised work will show the best current way to assemble, so the defect is less likely to be caused by the way the product was built.'

C: 'Excellent. Problems on the factory floor generally come from five areas: materials – the parts he's assembling together are faulty; method – the standard work isn't robust enough; machine – the machine or piece of equipment he's using isn't functioning as it should; man – your operator is creating the problem; or environment – something about the area is causing a problem, maybe ambient temperature or a draught or something else. If you've got strong, proven standardised work in place, which of those five can you rule out pretty quickly?'

J: 'Man… and method, I guess.'

C: 'That's right. Your problem solving becomes easier. But what about Markus in this case?'

J: 'Ah, I see. If he follows the standardised work and a problem happens he's fireproof and won't get in trouble.'

C: 'Exactly. When you come marching down the line to investigate the defect, Markus won't have a worried mind because the standard work is like an insurance policy in his back pocket. Now he has a personal reason to follow it.'

J: 'OK, I'll go tell him that.'

C: 'Not yet. You said he had some good knacks. Here, take your pretty, laminated Standardised Work and a pen and ask Markus about those couple of knacks that would improve it. Let him see you update it as you talk, then run it past the Engineer and reissue it... then have the conversation.'

6.4 Scenario 2: Catch many small fish, not one big one

Challenging the Western mindset

Heather – shown as H below – is a Senior Supervisor who is regularly on the end of a kicking from her Manager for not completing things, particularly kaizen projects. She starts but rarely finishes, and her people get fed up before they have even got half way.

H: 'It's got so bad that none of my team will come to me with ideas for anything to do with kaizen or sorting out our defects. They know that I want to finish things and make big improvements for them, but it's like they don't believe I can do it,' says Heather, gloomily.

Once again the coach is shown as C below.

C: 'How do they know you want to make big improvements for them?'
H: 'I've told them loads of times.'
C: 'Anything more than words?'
H: Defensively: 'I'm not just a talker, you know. I've tried doing loads of stuff, but it's not that easy.'
C: 'Good. Can you show me the last improvement idea from one of your team that you implemented...?'

Heather starts to speak.

C: '...and by implemented, I mean finished and proved it works.'

Big pause. Silence.

H: 'I've told you, they've stopped giving me ideas.'

C: Softly spoken: 'Why do you think that is?'
H: 'They seem to have lost faith. I think John has been stirring up trouble and...'
C: 'Heather, this isn't about John. It's about you. When did someone last come to you with an idea?'
H: 'Oh it's got to be a couple of months.'
C: 'Do you have it written down somewhere?'
H: 'Of course. I keep all of the kaizen ideas they come up with.'

She leads the coach to her Team Leader area and goes to a cabinet with pristine files labelled up. She pulls out a sheet with a list of kaizen ideas written on it.

C: 'It's good to see that you record the ideas. Out of interest, who typed these up?'
H: 'I did.'
C: 'OK, we'll come back to that. Take it out of the folder and pin it on the wall by the cell and we'll go through the last five.'
C: Indicating the most recent entry on the list: 'Whose idea was this and did it help?'

The question is repeated for each of the last five ideas. The answer is that three different associates gave those five ideas. One associate, Sue, came up with three of them. None of the 5 has been actioned yet. Heather explains: 'I told them that they'd be sorted when I make the big changes around the area.'

C: 'These are dated early April. It's July now.'
H: 'I know, I know, but like I say, I'm trying to finish this big layout change. Everything will be OK then.'
C: 'Fair play to Sue, she gave you three kaizen ideas. Put yourself in her

shoes for a minute. How many more would you offer up knowing that these three have been ignored?'

H: Protesting: 'They haven't been ignored!'

C: 'You've tried to implement them then?'

H: 'Well no, but I've thought about them.'

C: 'Then they've been ignored. For the last year I've been thinking about losing the extra stone I'm carrying, but I stand here today with my trousers still tight around my waist.'

H: 'I see what you're saying, but Sue knows me.'

C: 'What am I saying?'

H: 'That I should just get on with it... but I honestly haven't got time.'

C: 'When did you find time to type up these 20 odd kaizen ideas and file them away? That took time... wasted time. Typing up a kaizen sheet is pure waste. Spend the time sorting a problem, not making the explanation of the problem prettier.'

Heather nods grudging agreement.

C: 'Let's do this one now, the one about turning the jig around. We've got five minutes.'

The pair of them try turning the jig through 90º, having had a quick chat with Sue whose idea it was. She's happy to try out the new way for an hour.

C: 'Well done, Heather. What do you think?'

H: 'It's a nothing improvement. I can make a much bigger impact.'

C: Sharply. 'Where? Show me something you've changed in the last month that was bigger than what we've just achieved.'

Heather doesn't answer, but starts to unfold her big new layout plan.

C: 'Put that plan away for the minute. I've been planning to lose that stone in weight for the last 10 years. It's a great plan. What have you actually done? Did you see Sue's face when we left her?'
H: 'She looked happy enough.'
C: 'What's her cycle time? Fifty seconds?'

Heather nods.

C: 'So she's had to fight with that jig 600 times a day. It saves one second per cycle as well, which equals 10 minutes a day, 50 minutes a week, three-and-a-half hours a month, 40 hours a year. That's a week of Sue's time. Now tell me it's a nothing improvement. You have no credibility because you are not interested in your team's ideas. Ask for no more ideas until you've investigated and tried these old ones.'
H: 'I'm trying to make the big improvements that make a big difference to them.'
C: 'You're trying to catch a big fish, but that's not what kaizen is about.'
H: 'Fish?'
C: 'You ever been fishing Heather?'
H: 'No.'
C: 'Let me tell you about my grandfather. He was very keen on two things: fishing and telling stories. One story that has stayed with me concerns him and his friend who used to fish competitively. When you all gather around a lake or along a canal to fish, that's called a contest. They used to fish contests regularly and were good friends for years. They differed in one key respect though; their attitude to fishing.

My grandfather's friend would always set himself up to go for the biggest fish in the lake. That's the only one that interested him because he figured that he'd only have to catch the one to win the contest. So he'd prepare elaborately and strike out for that big fish, fishing in the most difficult parts of the lake. A familiar story would unfold as the contest went on. My grandfather would be pulling small fish out fairly regularly, his net slowly filling. Who do you think won more contests?'

H: 'Your granddad, I guess.'
C: 'That's right. It's basic maths. Six 2lb fish beats one 10lb fish. Of course, occasionally my grandfather's friend got lucky and pulled out the big fish, but these victories were few and far between. Most times, he would be biteless, get increasingly frustrated that the big fish eluded him and start blaming the world for his woes... the lake was badly stocked, the weather not right, he'd drawn a bad peg to fish from. What am I saying to you?'
H: 'I shouldn't be trying to make big improvements. But nobody in this company would complain if I delivered a big improvement. Surely the company needs me to make big improvements...'
C: 'Maybe so, if you actually delivered these improvements. This isn't about you though. I don't measure your ability by looking at you. I look at those who have worked for you for some time. Our company needs you to lead your people to show them how to catch fish – small ones at first. Imagine 10 fishermen gathered around a lake all pulling out small fish regularly. Soon, they'll far exceed the weight of any single fish.

Sure, sometimes needs must and a dramatic change is required in a crisis, but we only make kaizen a part of daily business by showing that it can be easy and quick, to build impetus and motivation. Your people think you're a lousy fisherman because you haven't proved you're not. All they've heard you do is bang on about perfect rig set-ups, sexy bait mixtures, the feeding habits of fish and river strategy.

Concentrate on catching small fish, hone your technique in the easier parts of the lake first. Your people will get confidence that you can do it and start asking you questions. By the way, my father used to go on those fishing trips, as did my grandfather's friend's son. Which one of those boys do you think developed an enjoyment and desire to continue fishing when every small catch or near miss was celebrated?'

6.5 Scenario 3: A chick waiting for a worm

Understanding the true nature of the problem

Simon (S), the Materials Planner, is making a hasty beeline for the coach (C) who is the General Manager. The coach likes to know what's going on in the plant and used to work in Materials. 'We're about to run out of boxes to put the Acme Ltd delivery in,' Simon blurts out. 'What shall we do?'

C: 'About to run out. What does that mean exactly?'
S: 'We're going to struggle on the next shipment.'
C: 'Come on, Simon, you know how this works. Give me better information.'
S: 'The 8pm shipment is short. The parts are scheduled to hit final assembly at 5.30.'
C: 'OK, so we have 2.5 hours to sort this.'
S: 'I don't want to cut it too fine.'
C: 'Clearly.' Then he falls silent. A big pause.
S: 'What shall we do then?'
C: 'What do you want to do?'
S: 'I don't know. That's why I've come to you.'
C: 'You want me to think for you?'
S: 'No, but...'
C: 'If I wasn't here, what would you do?'
S: 'I'd decant all of those'. Simon points to a pile of boxes. 'They're not needed until tomorrow.'
C: 'So why are you asking me what I think?'
S: 'All right, all right. I know the company doesn't like that because of the double handling and the risk of damage.'

C: 'Good. That idea's off the menu then. Do me a favour: take 15 minutes and think it through. I'll still be here and I do want you to come back.'

Simon leaves, not happy. Ten minutes pass before he returns.

S: 'OK. I've got two other options. We could ship the parts in non-standard boxes just this once and notify the customer or send the driver out to the customer to pick up some empties urgently. They're an hour away though, so it'd be tight.'
C: 'What are the pros and cons of each of those?'
S: 'The non-standard boxes sort the problem pretty quickly.'
C: 'Any drawbacks?'
S: 'Obviously, the customer won't be happy.'
C: 'Correct. We're not in the business of making our problem their problem.'

The discussion continues and the third option proves unpalatable as well.

S: 'I'm not being funny, but I've come to you with three courses of action and you've shot all three down. What do you expect me to do?'
Y: 'Solve the problem. How many times do I want you to solve this particular problem though?'
S: 'What do you mean?'
C: 'I'm honestly not trying to trick you. How many times do I want you to solve it?'
S: 'Once, obviously.'
C: 'True. Have you had this problem before?'
S: 'Yes, six weeks ago.'
C: 'How did you solve it that time?'
S: 'Decanting. Of course, you'd say we didn't solve it before because it's happened again today.'

C: 'Fair point. So, what did you miss last time?'

S: 'We didn't get to the bottom of it. Is this that root cause fish skeleton stuff you talk about?'

C: 'Root cause is the phrase I wanted to hear. Can you take me to the stores where you keep the boxes?'

In the stores area:

C: 'OK, step 1. What is the exact problem?'

S: 'We haven't got enough boxes.'

C: Pointing to the right: 'Are you sure? I can see plenty of empty boxes over there.'

S: Exasperated: 'We haven't got enough plastic boxes.'

C: Pointing to the left: 'Are those plastic over there? There are loads of them.'

S: 'ACME plastic boxes.'

C: 'Good, now we're getting more specific. So, we haven't got enough ACME plastic boxes. Correct?'

S: 'Yes.'

C: 'How many are you short?'

S: 'I'm not sure. My storeman just said he was short.'

C: Frowning: 'Please find out.'

Simon calls his storeman.

S: 'He says 53.'

C: 'I'm not convinced. Prove it.'

Simon does some maths on a scrap of paper to work out how many they need to service the stock in the loop to allow for lead-time, stock and delivery frequencies. He checks how many are officially on site, at the customer and in transit. Twenty more minutes have passed.

S: 'This is mad. We should have enough by my maths... I don't understand it.'

C: 'OK, so your problem has gone from "We haven't got enough boxes" to "We haven't got enough plastic ACME boxes available now". It's really important to tightly define your problem. What now?'

S: 'I need to find out where they all are.'

C: 'Correct. Come with me as time's running out.'

They go to the edge of the site behind the main warehouse. There sits a pile of ACME boxes, amongst others, gathering fetid rainwater.

C: 'Storeman mention those to you? I saw them the last time we ran out. You need to think about how you control and store the empties. Sort your shipment today, but tomorrow I want you to look into this. I'd like you to walk me round with a rough proposal on Friday.'

S: 'OK. I'll get these cleaned up. Thanks.'

C: 'Simon, next time you come to me with just a problem, no analysis and no suggested solutions, I'll give you a right going over. Bring me some facts and ideas and I'll happily help you work through them.'

6.6 Scenario 4: The map is not the territory

Understanding how others communicate

The coach (C) overhears a conversation between Al (A), one of his managers, and one of his direct reports, James (J) in Al's office. It appears to be hotting up and the coach listens to a minute or so, including the following:

J: 'I'm not stupid. I just can't see what you mean. I'm trying to picture it but I don't think it'll work.'
A: 'Listen, I've talked you through this several times. Pin back your ears because this is the last time.'
J: 'That's not fair...'

The coach hovers in the doorway and listens. The conversation quickly tails off.

C: 'Everything OK, fellas?'

Both shrug.

C: 'Tell you what James; can you give Al and me a minute? I'm sure Al will come and see you straight after we've finished to resolve this.'
J: 'Oh. OK.'

James leaves and Al stays

C: 'Do you want a hand with this Al?'
A: 'Yeah. I've been talking to a brick wall.'
C: 'I heard a bit of your conversation... tell me what it was all about.'

Al starts to explain, but you interrupt:

C: 'Sorry, Al, there's something interesting in what I'm hearing. I'd like to write up on the board what was said. Can I write what you said in blue and what he said in red?'

Al nods warily. You write up half a dozen sentences of the conversation, including those in the description of the scenario above.

C: 'Stand back and look at the words Al. I'm going to take a punt here and guess that you can generally understand something from a good explanation. In fact, you prefer this to being shown something?'
A: 'Yes, doesn't everybody?'
C: 'No, in fact I'll bet that James doesn't. The problem here is that you two experience the world differently and probably learn things differently.'
A: 'How did you know I prefer to listen rather than look?'
C: 'There are some clues in the words you use. Here, I'll underline a few of them.'

The coach underlines 'listen', 'talked' and 'pin back your ears' in blue followed by 'see' and 'picture' in red.

A: 'Well, will you look at that. Not sure it helps me though.'
C: 'James's words are to do with seeing and yours are to do with listening. Both of you experience the world through your eyes, ears, touch, taste and smell, but most people have a dominant sense that helps them make sense of the world, normally either visual (eyes obviously), auditory (ears) or kinaesthetic (touch) dominates.

James' words suggest that he understands best when he can visualise something. Frequent use of words like 'see' and 'picture' give a clue. With practice, you can even observe how people breathe and their eye movements to give clues about how they experience the world.'

A: 'I still can't see how it helps me.'
C: 'Listen. Good communication is built on rapport. You'll get a lot further if the person you're talking to feels that you understand something about them, have something in common with them, particularly if you're selling an improvement idea like you were today. Most importantly, it's easier for him to understand if you talk his language.

The fact that James can't grasp, see or hear the benefit of what you're saying at the moment is your failure in communication, not his. You need to join him in his map of the world, in a manner of speaking.'

A: 'So I need to talk in words that are visual.'
C: 'That would be a good step. What else might work even better?'
A: 'I could draw him a diagram?'
C: 'Good, that's even better. Or go one step further and show him. Help him 'picture it' and then you'll understand whether he's objecting because he doesn't understand or because he sees a flaw in the plan. Either way, you can't lose.'

6.7 Scenario 5: The answer's no, now what's the question?

How to earn understanding and challenge your assumptions

An engineer, Lou (L) comes to the coach (C) with a layout for a new manufacturing cell. He talks the coach through the layout, but insists that he needs one extra person to feed kits of material into the assembly end of the cell. The coach notices a very big rack in the middle of the cell between the fabrication and assembly end of the cell where the kits are assembled.

C: 'Thanks for the walk-through, Lou. How many people are needed to run the area?'
L: 'Twelve.'
C: 'How many people should there be?'
L: Looks slightly confused: 'Er, I need 12.'
C: 'That's the answer to a different question. What is the costed manpower for the new cell?'
L: 'Eleven, I think, but I can check later.'
C: 'Check now, please... unless you're planning to fund the extra person from your wages?'
L: Smiles awkwardly. 'OK. I just need to nip back to the office.'

He leaves and returns several minutes later.

L: 'It should be 11.'
C: 'So why are you asking me for 12? If I give you 12 without questioning it, we make a loss on this product from the very beginning. No matter how well you lay the area out, we'll be playing catch-up. Better to accept the headache now and kaizen before you bolt anything down. So, how

many people are needed?'

L: 'Eleven... but I need to find a way to get to 11 from 12.'

C: 'Now we're talking. How much time do you need to save to get to the 11?'

Lou does the calculation.

C: 'OK. So what ideas have you got?'

L: 'I've tried a lot of things. The extra person is to double up on line feeding the area. I've timed it to see how long it takes to cover the ground.' He adds hastily: 'I've done the analysis.'

C: 'Good. Let's have a look at your work combination table.'

L: 'I haven't done that yet, but I've timed 10 cycles of the line feeder job and tried to move things in closer. I can go away and do that, though.'

C: 'No need. We'll simulate it now. You be the line feeder. As you go, shout out what you're doing and I'll time you and write the elements down. I'm assuming that these tape marks on the floor are where things are going to go?'

L: 'Yes.'

C: 'What's this area going to be?' pointing to a large taped rectangle on the floor.

L: 'The subassembly bench and rack.'

C: 'OK, let's crack on.'

They run the simulation several times.

C: 'Make this the last cycle now; I think I've captured everything. Take a look at this, Lou. What do you notice from these timings?'

L: Pointing to the chart: 'The bulk of the time is collecting the upper case parts.'

C: 'Why's that?'

L: 'I was having to walk back and forth to fill the kit... from there to there.'

C: 'Were you taking the most direct route?'

L: 'No. I knew that the subs bench and rack were in the way, but didn't realise it took so much time to get round.'

C: 'Why is the subs bench and rack in that spot?'

L: 'I know what you're going to say, but I've tried it and it won't work.'

C: 'Listen, I'll spend time on this with you but I have a few rules. The quickest way to see me walk away is to say something like you just have. I don't want to hear "The answer's no, now what's the question?" Let's take this a step at a time. Why are the upper case parts over there and not closer?'

L: 'Because I can't put them any closer.'

C: 'Why not?'

L: 'I have the subs bench and rack here.'

C: 'Where are the subs fitted?'

L: Pointing: 'Over there.'

C: 'So there's no flow reason why the bench and rack are here. Why are they here, then?'

L: 'It's the only place I could fit them.'

C: Looking at the times you wrote down from the simulation: 'Getting this subs bench and rack out of the way would give you 60% of your required time saving, wouldn't it?'

L: 'Looks that way.'

C: 'Let's try it.'

L: 'No point, they're too big to fit anywhere else.'

C: Smiling: 'You've done it again. Second strike! Just for that I'm telling you that this bench and rack have to go in that space at the edge there.'

L: Protesting: 'But they won't fit.'

C: 'How can you make something big fit into a small space? Give me a simple answer, not an engineering solution.'

L: 'Make it smaller.'
C: 'Good. Do me a favour, measure the space you've marked out for the rack only.'

It turns out to be 3m x 2m.

C: 'So that's 6 square metres. OK, now measure the bench space.'
It measures 1m x 1.5m.
C: 'Now. Let's drag a bench in to fill that space. Assemble one for me, would you?'

Lou does so.

C: 'Thanks. I'll do one now. Keep an eye on how much of the bench I'm using.'
Assembles the parts comfortably, but uses about a third of the bench surface.

C: 'Got a hacksaw?'
L: 'OK. So that saves me a bit, but that's not enough yet, and besides, I give him a bit of extra space in case he wants to put something down.'
C: 'Like what? There's the defect box over there and he should only be working on one piece at a time. Never give any more flat surfaces than are strictly needed. They'll get filled with something.'
L: 'What about the rest of the rack?'
C: 'Well, by my maths, you've got half a square metre of value added space with 6 square metres of racking to support. What do you think about that ratio?'
L: 'It's poor, I know, but I need it to hold the stock.'
C: 'Tell me what my next question is going to be?'
L: 'Why have I got so much stock on the rack?'

C: 'Nearly, but I'd be presuming that there's too much without the facts.'
L: Tries again, hopefully: 'How much stock is on there?'
C: 'Bingo.'
L: 'Same as before, but before you ask I'll count it.'

He works it out to two days' worth.

C: 'How often is it replenished?'
L: 'Should be every three hours, but sometimes they don't come on time...'
C: 'That's a different problem. Don't hide that problem here or we'll never flush it out to solve it. Even so, how often are they one-and-a-half days late?'
L: 'Never.'
C: 'You could cut that space in half right here and now couldn't you. We've found the first 60%. The rest is up to you. You've got a good mind, Lou, but you don't challenge the status quo enough.'

The coach slaps him on the back and walks away.

6.8 To a man with a hammer, everything looks like a nail

That's pretty much how those conversations played out. The resolutions were neither right nor wrong. They were, however, useful in that they challenged each of the individuals to find a better way. All five of the scenarios had a fair degree of leading, probing and questioning, but not much answer-giving. The difficulty of taking a questioning approach is hard to grasp until you try it. See how long it is until you blurt out the answer or, at the least, a firm direction. Therein lies our collective failing.

We picture a capable manager as one who dispenses quickfire solutions in the eye of the storm. 'Do this. Ask that. Find out this.' It feels good, but does nothing to improve another's skill. Nothing grows in the shadow of the mighty oak. Your team end up like chicks in the nest waiting for the worm to be dropped into their mouth.

The next time someone asks you a question to solve a problem they have, consider simply saying:

'What do you think?' and follow the thread from there for a pretty handy win:win.

It gets your people thinking, you might learn something and, rather usefully, if you do not know the answer it buys you time. A word of caution though: don't try it during a real crisis and don't blindly ask: 'Why?' The skill is in leading the discussion the right way: blind whys are lazy and will only serve to infuriate.

Which would you rather be during the prolonged storm and bad weather we face in business today: the oak tree that gets torn out of the ground by the force of the wind or the reed that yields to the direction of the wind and is, thus, able to withstand the onslaught? Coaching lean leaders is all about flexibility of thought in dealing with challenges.

I saw a good example in the paper recently. It read as follows: *'A Bangkok fireman dressed up as Spiderman to rescue an eight-year-old boy from a window ledge. The boy, who is autistic, had a panic attack on his first day at school, and crawled out of the third-floor window. Neither teachers nor rescue workers could coax him back in, until his mother mentioned his passion for comic superheroes. Fireman Somchai Yoosabai rushed back to his station, where he keeps a Spiderman costume to liven up school fire drills. At the sight of his favourite superhero, the boy broke into a huge smile and flung himself into Yoosabai's arms.'*

A little known law of cybernetics, Ashby's law of requisite variety, makes the same fundamental point a different way. Ashby's law states that – forget cybernetics and think about people – the person with the greatest flexibility of thought and behaviour tends to control the outcome of any interaction between people. Now that sounds a pretty useful skill.

Finally, some of the most powerful guidance I have received involved very few words. Most of that early guidance came from my Sensei, Toshiyuki Muraoka, a Toyota veteran, who we'll hear a lot from in the final chapter of this book. I once spent a day with a team of operators, team leaders and maintenance men improving the 5s condition of an area by the usual means. The area I had chosen was too big to improve to any depth, but we had rushed to get the tape down on the floor at the end. I was very proud of having got the job done. I asked Muraoka-san as he wandered past at the end of the day:

'What do you think?'

This was one time I did not need our interpreter:

'Pretty,' he said, without a smile.

I got his point immediately. Any more words would have been a waste. That one word was far less than the daily hour or so debriefs we usually had. He knew that saying any more would dilute the lesson. A flexible reed indeed.

Chapter 7

The Lean You - Clear Thinking

"Time is the shadow of motion"

7.1 The T in TPS also stands for thinking

Teruyuki Minoura has been a Senior Executive in the Toyota Group of companies for many years. Beyond this fairly pedestrian fact I know little about him; and that little I gleaned from a global purchasing article dated 2003. In common with most people, I rarely remember the intricacies of 8 year old articles. This one though, contained a phrase that jumped off the page at me. Minoura-san stated "The T in TPS also stands for thinking". Genius.

Such genius, in fact, that the lion's share of this chapter is about just that word; thinking. More specifically, the need to think clearly and scientifically to help your Lean business survive in this Lean world.

I have been thinking about time a lot recently, particularly how poorly I have been using my own. This reflection plagued me as I ploughed through another week of rising at 05.30 hrs to the dawning realisation that I had work to do for one customer before I could go to work for another that morning! I can't be alone here...

The perception that to be busy is to be productive may be at the heart of this. Unfortunately, challenging how people use their time is not for the faint hearted; the blood of the questioner can quickly be drawn in response. Questioning time usage is often perceived as a thinly cloaked accusation of laziness or daftness.

Is time more relevant now than in the past? Chapter three discussed practical ways to bolster your business to cope during recessionary times. Given the depth of the recent downturn, many of you may now find yourselves having to either:

Do less or the same amount of work with proportionally fewer people – that is, where a 20% cut in sales orders may, unfortunately, result in a 20% cut in direct, indirect and support staff, the workload may not fall prorata; or,

Do more; even those businesses where volumes are holding or growing are likely feeling a reticence to take on more people (and introduce more fixed cost to the business thus raising the break-even point), so that the same number of employees have to handle more work.

Whichever of these camps you are currently in, it strikes me that time has become an even more relevant issue now. The job still has to get done. During the last few years, I have spent a lot of my days working with directors, managers and supervisors, training and coaching them to control their part of the business better and squeeze some ongoing improvement out of it. When starting to work with a new supervisor or manager, a common theme surfaces rapidly: the lack of time to do what they currently do, let alone anything extra.

All of these people understand and embrace the need to improve the business. They are often simply frustrated by an inability to find the necessary time to do it. A part of the problem, I believe, is a tacit assumption that most of the things that currently fill their time are all valuable. This assumption is reflected in the complaint that a kitchen cupboard, garage or a handbag even, is too small. The issue is often not a lack of space or capacity, but that the space is being filled with the wrong things.

Disagree? Can I ask you to stop reading now and take a stroll to your kitchen cupboard that houses the baked beans, tinned tomatoes, etc. If it is full, do a quick and dirty 5s sort and segregate the items into: 1, those that are out of date; 2, those that have not been touched for some weeks (blow the dust off the labels); and 3, those that are current. For this final group, consider your inventory levels. If you were to put only the essential things back into the cupboard in sensible quantities, hey presto, you have a bigger cupboard. There is a self-defeating futility to spending money to buy a bigger briefcase or handbag that will soon be filled.

Now substitute time for cupboard space. One particular team leader I work with had to spend an hour a day recording how his shift had performed on three different sets of paperwork – that is, the same information on different formats. He certainly struggled for time! Would anybody out there like to suggest a solution to his simple problem? Interestingly, he was a smart man who had simply grown accustomed to doing something. In effect it had become mental and muscle memory.

7.2 Challenge yourself

I am sure a number of you can identify with this experience. The following story from Shigeo Shingo's book *Key Strategies for Plant Improvement* is interesting:

'A scientist once performed an experiment to see whether goldfish could remember things. First he built a glass tank with a glass barrier in the middle; in the centre of the barrier he made a hole large enough for a goldfish to swim through. When he placed a goldfish on one side of the barrier and food on the other side, the goldfish headed straight for the food and ran into the transparent pane of glass. After repeating this action a number of times, the goldfish managed to pass through the central hole to the food. After numerous repetitions, the goldfish would head straight through the hole and eat the food. Next, the researcher removed the glass barrier and placed the trained goldfish on one side of the tank and food on the other side. In spite of the fact that the barrier was gone, the goldfish still swam to the food via the place where the hole had been. In other words, force of habit led the goldfish to persist in its old behaviour despite a change in the situation.'

Systems and procedures often evolve over time and become a part of the daily pattern without being challenged. Now is the time to challenge. To cite a lack of time without an honest appraisal of how you currently fill it should be met with short shrift.

If we have a bottleneck station on an assembly line, we analyse it to see the waste/muda and then remove it. We focus on the value-added. Surely, this sort of critical analysis should operate throughout the business at management levels, not just on the shop floor, in the hospital wards, the airport baggage handling area or those working the phones in a call centre, where work is more tangible and easier to study.

As management, we surely have a responsibility to look for waste/muda in what we do and standardise a proportion of our day as far as is useful? Choosing any other path is to become the kind of manager who subconsciously says to his people: 'Do as I say, not as I do.'

Our long-deceased economist friend Pareto has something to say here. If we truly believe the Pareto principle – and statistics broadly bear it out – then 80% of our good activities – *value adding or value creating*, see below for an explanation – will come from 20% of the things we do. Does this mean that the 80% comes from what we do for only two of our ten hours a day? Are all the tasks that fill the other eight hours meaningless?

I doubt it. A proportion is probably *non-value adding/creating* leaving a hefty rump of pure *waste or muda*. Whilst I am not about to launch into a messianic rant on the benefits of time management – I am not a practising expert! – I am arguing that we all look at how we use the time available to us. There is a particular Chinese adage that suggests that 'life unfolds on a great sheet called time, and once finished it is gone forever'.

7.3 Not all work is valuable

One of my Toyota mentors put it slightly differently in reminding me that one day is 24 hours. Time is the resource that everybody in this world shares together and equally. The difference is in how you choose to use these hours for best effect. It is widely agreed that a careful observation of work in any environment reveals three categories of activity. Traditionally, in a lean environment, these have been labelled:

1. Value-added work: activities that change the nature, shape or characteristics of the product towards what the customer wants, and is willing therefore to pay for – for example, the moment that a bolt being fitted to an assembly becomes torqued up.

2. Non-value-added work: activities that do not add value but have to be done, under current conditions, to allow us to add value – for example, picking up the bolt from a pot situated conveniently for you and starting to tighten it.

3. Waste or muda: everything else – such as having to walk and/or reach for the bolt. Using a bolt that has too many thread turns or having to use a worn out wrench on the bolt that rounds the head off and keeps slipping. It follows that the aim is to maximise the value-added, minimise the non-value-added and eliminate the waste/muda.

The perfect working day would be filled exclusively with value-added activities. The distinctions are similar but not quite so clear cut in healthcare or financial services, but nonetheless, value still resides in the eye of the beholder, the customer. Value-creating activities in a healthcare setting might be those that the customer judges of value – that is, curing an illness, reducing pain, giving preventative care, etc.

In the UK we pay our taxes for an NHS that promises universal access to healthcare free at the point of delivery. I will conveniently skirt the private finance initiatives and choice debates here. Consider surgeons working in theatres. Theatres are generally scarce, capacity restrained, expensively kitted resources with significant running costs. An expert team needs to be assembled to perform an operation.

Is it fair to say that an example of value-added here is the time the surgeon spends with a scalpel in his or her hand operating on you? Is scrubbing up time non-value-added, assuming the facilities are good and available? Is having the wrong sterilised tool available or a surgeon waiting outside a theatre for an over-running operation to finish an example of waste/muda? What category does consultation and diagnosis fall into? Correct diagnoses are surely valuable. Either way, the principles are similar.

Of course, from a manager's perspective, nothing that we do adds value as we do not physically transform any products or treat patients or prepare the meals for in-flight. Conversely, we are clearly not useless as we marshal, plan, co-ordinate and confirm. The key point is that our job is to decide how best to support those who are directly adding value and take those activities that are difficult or tricky to perform and make them easy for the value-adders to do, repeatedly, in a pressured environment.

So, this may be a good point to start from. Which of the tasks, performed each day, directly supports either the value-adders or the customer in ways that he or she is prepared to pay for? Below is a list of questionable examples that have presented themselves to me recently:

- A supervisor, one of 15 in this specific business, who spends 1.5 hours every morning collecting information on the previous 24 hour performance for **his** manager to report to **his** Director in a 30-minute meeting.

- A conversation with a manager who spent about an hour typing up a list of problems we had found by looking at an area because the handwritten list did not look right. He could have spent the time solving several of the problems on the list – which was legible and live! The subconscious message this can send is that you need a computer to make improvements!

- An overworked lady in a purchasing department who spent a fair portion of her day chasing people to get them to fill in the parts of the form that they had missed out first time: defects by another name. It had not occurred to her to train them – nobody had.

- Five different team leaders who every morning walk several hundred yards to a stores area and manually count the stock in there because they do not trust the warehouse or the computer. This waste/muda task takes even longer because the stock is not labelled or segregated.

- Lateness to arrive at meetings. Eleven people waiting for one person five minutes late equals one hour. I know one Production Director who locks the door at the start time and waves away latecomers. Dyson, the vortex hoover people in Malmesbury, apparently had no chairs in meeting rooms and the tables were at navel height, figuring that a person in mild discomfort is more likely to be succinct.

Once I have challenged and solved my own 'simple examples', I will be looking at where I spend the lion's share of my remaining working time, and apply the principle that 'time is the shadow of motion' – that is, the length of time something takes is not the cause of it taking a long time, but merely the effect.

If I want to speed things up, working faster is the wrong answer. I need to attack the activities that cast the shadow of time and take waste/muda out of them. As a final point, I read last year a comment from a man who answered a simple interview question in an enlightening way. The question he was asked by the interviewer interested in his profession was 'what is your job?'

His answer: 'My job is to improve the way I do my job.' Job done.

7.4 Snatching defeat from the jaws of victory

One balmy April afternoon in 2009, to, I suspect, raucous cheers in Cordoba, Angel Cabrera won golf's US Masters in Augusta. His playoff victory ensured that he became the first ever Argentinian to win the coveted green jacket that proclaims victory in the Masters, one of golf's major competitions. He could, and probably should, have been the second Argentinian to win it, but for the simple error committed by countryman Roberto De Vicenzo almost a year before Cabrera was born.

The year was 1968 and De Vicenzo is a man for whom the phrase 'snatching defeat from the jaws of victory' could have been invented. To tell the story, I place you briefly in the hands of Rick Dorsey, a staff writer for CNN Sports Illustrated:

It appeared that De Vicenzo, who was celebrating his 45th birthday during Sunday's final round, would be heading toward a playoff with Bob Goalby after both players had finished with apparent 11-under 277s. The playoff never materialized. While players of today and yesterday keep each other's score during competitive rounds, electronic scoring is today's fallback measure.

De Vicenzo had no such fail-proof mechanism, so he signed his scorecard, kept by his playing partner that day Tommy Aaron. Unbeknownst to the happy-go-lucky Argentine, Aaron had credited him with a par 4 on the 17th when in reality, De Vicenzo had tallied a birdie 3. When he penned his fateful signature, De Vicenzo still fumed at hooking his drive at the 18th and knocking his approach clear over the green. Instead of the meticulous scrutiny needed to correct Aaron's scoring faux pas, De Vicenzo trumped the blunder by glancing over his card and agreeing to the wrong score. USGA rules indicate that if a competitor returns a score higher than actually played, it must stand as returned.

'I look at card, and all I see was my score on 16 and that I made five on 18,' De Vicenzo would say later.
Tournament officials quickly huddled about the inconceivable dilemma that confronted them. They stood by the rules, promptly handing the championship to Goalby, who turned in a correct scorecard.

Dorsey closes the article by recounting the five words uttered by Vicenzo when he learned of his error:

'What a stupid I am.'

Here are two related facts to kick us off:

Somewhere in England there lives a man who runs a mid-sized Toyota car dealership. This man would never tire of hitting me.

My wife drives a Toyota Corolla Verso. The front wheel of this very reliable, safe and well-built car is central to this story.

Exactly how these two facts are related to the De Vicenzo story will become clear. My own 'snatching defeat from the jaws of victory' story is laid out below by way of an email exchange with the General Manager of the dealership mentioned above. One of my many character flaws is that, very occasionally, I descend a little hastily into obnoxiousness in the face of poor service. Believe me, I have worked on this over the years, but my wife will attest that there is some way to go before I'll be passing time meditating under ice cold waterfalls reciting impenetrable Zen riddles with the ghost of a smile playing upon my lips.

Laying bare my personal angst, for all to see, is not generally my style, but I make an exception here. Several interesting problem-solving and scientific management points of note arise from the discussion below. Received wisdom within the lean community is that the ability to problem-solve logically and simply is one of, and maybe the critical technical management skill.

Whilst reading, please forgive my flashes of obnoxiousness; the replies were often dashed off via my Blackberry whilst either working or sitting up in bed, without much forethought. In the interests of integrity, I reveal the emails verbatim even though, in tone, some of my comments are wince inducing.

Ironically enough, the story begins on Friday 13th March 2009. My wife had been experiencing a grinding/graunching noise whilst driving her car and decided to call the RAC upon reaching her destination. The reason for the noise becomes apparent below if you have the iron will to reach the end of this exchange.

From: russell.watkins@xxxxxx
To: Service Manager – Toyota Dealership
Sent: Friday, March 13, 2009 10:34 PM
Subject: Poor after sales response after safety concern

We met briefly in your office a week ago. 2 weeks ago your service department sent out my wife's car with 4 loose wheel nuts. Fortunately the RAC man discovered the problem before the wheel came off during driving. I am sure you remember this.
By way of apology you, and your colleague, offered us the next service free. This was going to be put in writing to us. No letter has arrived.

We explained to you how important it was that you perform a thorough investigation and root cause analysis of the problem to prevent recurrence. You told us how seriously you took the problem. We have heard nothing. I would be surprised if, as the after sales manager, you expected US to contact YOU to find out the result of your investigation.

My wife could have been injured or worse if that wheel had come off and I am left with the distinct impression that we left your mind as soon as we drove away. Put yourself in our shoes and ask whether this is the level of attention and response you would expect from an after sales manager in response to a safety issue. Please do not contact me personally as I will struggle to have confidence in whatever you tell me. Instead we would like your Dealer Principal to contact us with the result of the investigation.

As stated in your office, we don't believe the mechanic to be at fault as, in line with Toyota thinking, it is the process that has failed NOT the mechanic.

I look forward to receiving a call from your Dealer Principal on Monday.

Russell Watkins

Date: Mon, 16 Mar 2009 11:18:27
To: russell.watkins@xxxxxx
From: General Manager – Toyota Dealership
Subject: FW: Poor after sales response after safety concern

Dear Sir

I am writing in response to your request below regarding the after sales incident that occurred with your wife's car. I have discussed the sequence of events and your subsequent concern at length with (Service Manager – Toyota Dealership) this morning and I must apologise for you not having received a written communication regarding this subject earlier. It does appear that (Service Manager – Toyota Dealership), before confirming any action, was waiting for your final comments following your visit to his office. I do, however, realise that we should have contacted you having not heard anything.

In summary, I understand that the wheel nuts on your vehicle had worked loose following a service, and you rightfully brought this to our attention and questioned our process. We do have a quality check carried out on a percentage of the jobs carried out each day to try to ensure that this type of incident is avoided but on this occasion your vehicle was not subject to this check. I can assure you that incidents of this type are taken seriously and processes questioned, which in this case has been done. We do endeavour to check as much of our work each day in line with industry best practice and have independent statistics compiled to ensure adherence to this type of programme. This does not avoid every incident as your own experience shows and in recognition of that we have offered to carry out your next service free of charge. This, we also recognise, does not avoid the situation that occurred but does offer a goodwill gesture to recompense the inconvenience that was caused.

Please be assured that I am available to discuss the situation, should you believe it necessary, but I hope that this E Mail gives you the comfort that the matter has been taken seriously and at the right level.
Assuring you of prompt attention at all times

General Manager – Toyota Dealership

From: russell.watkins@xxxxxx

To: General Manager – Toyota Dealership
Sent: 17 March 2009 13:37
Subject: Re: Poor after sales response after safety concern

Are you absolutely sure that the best response you can give me is that; if our car is included in the small percentage of jobs you quality check we can rest easy. Does this mean that, if we are unlucky enough not to be in this random sample, we have to take our chances?

I was very clear with (Service Manager – Toyota Dealership) that I wanted to understand the root cause of this problem and the countermeasure that came from his investigation. Additionally, we have still received no letter and your email makes no reference to it.

It is your absolute right not to inform me of the details of your investigation (remember: it is the process weakness I am interested in, the mechanic is not to blame and we have no problem with him) but I am seriously considering contacting Toyota Sales UK for their view on the thoroughness of your investigation. The reason for this is that my wife and kids could have been seriously injured if we hadn't spotted the problem. I want to know what you will do to avoid this recurring. This is the Toyota way.

Date: Tue, 17 Mar 2009 14:23:12
To: russell.watkins@xxxxxx
From: General Manager – Toyota Dealership
Subject: RE: Poor after sales response after safety concern

Dear Sir

I think that I have been very clear in my previous E Mail that we have a process where vehicles are quality checked, and stated that this is through a random sample method in line with industry standard. From this it is clear that as your vehicle was not checked a fault could occur which then was the case, again not in dispute. I do think that this is serious and agree that this could have resulted in a terrible outcome, fortunately it did not. I am sure that having re visited our process that we have to look at quality checking a greater sample of jobs.

With regard to receiving a letter, I can confirm that following our correspondence and a satisfactory outcome this will be followed up in writing. Should you wish to take the matter up with Toyota Great Britain this is entirely within your prerogative.

In closing I want to assure you that I have given this matter priority recognising its importance and can only apologise for the event occurring in the first place. I do hope that our new process of more checks will ensure that it does not occur again.

Regards

General Manager – Toyota Dealership
From: russell.watkins@xxxxxx
To: General Manager – Toyota Dealership
Sent: 17 March 2009 14:35
Subject: Re: Poor after sales response after safety concern

Thank you for your prompt reply. I have to consider the possibility that I may have been unclear so I'll ask again: what was the root cause of the problem please?

Date: Tue, 17 Mar 2009 15:01:03
To: russell.watkins@xxxxxx

From: General Manager – Toyota Dealership
Subject: RE: Poor after sales response after safety concern

The root cause of the problem is that our sample size may not be large enough, to spot all possibilities, although it is higher than the industry average. There is not a 100% Quality check carried out on all jobs and this could lead to something being missed. Your particular job was carried out by a Senior technician who is one of the Quality Controllers. We have investigated possible causes of the defect and improved the process above.

Regards

General Manager – Toyota Dealership

From: russell.watkins@xxxxxx
To: General Manager – Toyota Dealership
Sent: 18 March 2009 22:05
Subject: Re: Poor after sales response after safety concern

Thanks again for the reply and please don't think I am being troublesome in my responses. I feel there is an important point here that you are missing.

It is the difference between spotting a problem (detection) and stopping it happening in the first place (prevention). The Toyota preference is for prevention rather than detection for obvious reasons. The root cause you stated is a failure in detection. I am only interested in how you prevent this same problem from happening in the first place. The only unattractive alternative is to inspect every car after any piece of work...there is clearly no business case for this.

Imagine I am a circus high wire walker, traversing a thin wire 50 feet up in a big top. Let's say I am lucky enough to have a safety net underneath in 10% of the venues I perform in. If I fall off the wire one night and break both legs on the ground below I have clearly been unfortunate. The root cause is NOT the lack of a safety net that night. It might have been that the wire was strung too loose OR I used the wrong balancing pole OR my shoes were too worn and the sole failed.

Either way, we won't stop me falling off again by having safety nets in more of the venues. The root cause is not that your sample size was not big enough, so what was it?

Regards

Date: Thu, 19 Mar 2009 10:01:13
To: russell.watkins@xxxxxx
From: General Manager – Toyota Dealership
Subject: RE: Poor after sales response after safety concern

Dear Mr Watkins

I do not think you are troublesome and I do not think that you believe I do not understand the difference between detection and prevention. The root cause as you say was the fact that somebody either did not tighten the wheel nuts to the correct torque or that somebody loosened them. It is impossible to know which of those was the cause. Assuming that they were not to the right torque when they left here the cause was that the mechanic did not set the torque correctly, something that has not occurred before by this technician. The tools are regularly calibrated and have been checked since to ensure that there was no fault. This is the case.

I am unable to satisfy your concern any more than above as this is as much information that I am able to give you. I can again only apologise for the situation arising and assure you that steps have been taken with process and technician interview to ensure that is unlikely to occur again.

Best regards

General Manager – Toyota Dealership

From: russell.watkins@xxxxxx
To: General Manager – Toyota Dealership
Sent: 25 March 2009 21:00
Subject: RE: Poor after sales response after safety concern

General Manager – Toyota Dealership,

Apologies for the delay. We are getting closer but, here is my 'remote' investigation...Toyota style. My only problem is that I haven't seen your service area so am lacking 'genchi genbutsu'.

The problem was 5 loose wheel nuts on the same wheel. The other 3 wheels had no problem. The problem wasn't discovered until some days after leaving your garage when a loud noise developed, a delay which suggests that they were, at least, hand-tight or pre-final torque and weren't completely loose when they left your garage. The RAC man confirms that because ALL 5 were loose it is unlikely to have been a natural working loose and we can rule out tampering by another party in the intervening period (because the locking wheel nut was also loose).

So, it was caused either by man, machine, material or method of service (we'll rule out environmental factors as there were no big weather swings during the period). MAN appears unlikely as you stated that he was an experienced service technician who is also a QA checker...so we'll rule out insufficient training and intentional undertorquing.

MACHINE refers to the tools he was using. I was pleased that you checked the torque settings of his spanner and assume he only uses the one spanner for wheel nuts of this kind. If it were a spanner issue I'd expect all 20 wheel nuts to be affected OR (if an intermittent fault) a random number of the 20. Five on one hub for an intermittent spanner problem is statistically extremely unlikely.

MATERIAL would suggest that the wheel hub itself or the threaded spigots or the nuts were at fault. This is unlikely as they have stayed in place since the RAC man tightened them with no repeat of the issue. I have checked this.

Which leaves us with METHOD i.e. the sequence or way in which the service was done. I'll assume you work to a check list and a skilled technician wouldn't normally have an issue as it's almost muscle memory for him. The key word is 'NORMALLY'.

Toyota belief is that most defects and accidents happen after 'change points'. Change points could be new tools, a new technician, interruption during a job...I'm guessing that your technician was interrupted or distracted after torquing 3 wheels (maybe to answer a query or help someone out) and when he came back he had lost his place and thus unknowingly skipped the fourth.

This is guesswork but it is the kind of investigation I expected from you. You'll understand why I was annoyed and deeply concerned to be told that the root cause was that our car wasn't in the checking sample. Let's remember that you and I both had a lucky escape. I still have my family and your company is not being sued for negligence in the death of a young family. This is why I have persisted in our discussion.

I'd like to offer a countermeasure to avoid recurrence. The Japanese Toyota supplier that I am currently consulting to has a good, clear, simple way to avoid this kind of problem. An operator cannot leave the line halfway through a cycle normally. If, however, he must leave the line or cell halfway through a cycle of work, he has a small laminated label he puts on the product he is building, this has the key steps printed on it and he can circle (with a dry wipe marker) the last stage he was at. When he comes back, there is no mistake.

Your Thoughts?

Date: 26/03/2009 13:11
To: russell.watkins@xxxxxx
From: General Manager – Toyota Dealership
Cc: Service Manager – Toyota Dealership
Subject RE: Poor after sales response after safety concern

Russell

Service Manager – Toyota Dealership tells me that this is a solution that both you and he discussed previously. Following your suggestion he did in fact consult with our workshop controller and we have introduced a mirror hanger which is placed in a vehicle should a technician be called from a job. This does the same thing reminding them where they are up to but in a written format.

I trust that this is what you would have expected us to do, but it is not one of our practices to inform customers of this type of follow up, maybe it should be.

Assuring you of my personal attention

General Manager – Toyota Dealership

From: russell.watkins@xxxxxx
To: General Manager – Toyota Dealership
Cc: Service Manager – Toyota Dealership
Sent: 02/04/2009 21:42
Subject: RE: Poor after sales response after safety concern

General Manager – Toyota Dealership,

Last conversation now. I am tired of going in circles with you. Your comments below are disingenuous at best. You are correct in that I suggested this countermeasure to Service Manager – Toyota Dealership as a possible at our first meeting (but that was a possible based on little investigation). I asked you OUTRIGHT two or three times (review the email trail please) what the root cause and countermeasure was. After some weak answers such as 'The root cause of the problem is that our sample size may not be large enough' we are now at the point where you have the gall to say 'it is not one of our practices to inform customers of this type of follow up'. I asked you OUTRIGHT several times. Did it not occur to you that this was the information I was after?

You are clearly not a fool but neither am I. I am smart enough to spot an evasive attempt to treat me like a fool. I await your letter confirming that our next service is free but please be aware that your understanding of investigation and root cause analysis falls well short of that expected by

Toyota as a manufacturing business. This should be a source of deep concern and reflection for you as you are the most customer facing part of the Toyota supply chain.

There the email trail ends.

You will notice that, to his credit, the General Manager was polite and businesslike all the way through. I have no concern with him, as my gripe is with the system that trains him. Toyota has gone to the trouble of building a high quality car that has served the Watkins family with a near unblemished record. Fine minds have designed the product, factory, machines and management systems that produced the car. Those same minds work daily to ensure that people within Toyota factories worldwide understand and live the Toyota Way to ensure jikoutei kanketsu – built-in quality with ownership.

The irony is that, as the end-customer, I never get to meet these people to experience first-hand the investment that has been made in them and their facility. On the other hand, twice a year I get to meet my Toyota dealership staff who are always unfailingly courteous and competent – right up until the point that an abnormal condition occurs, like my wife's wheel nuts. I have no doubt that I could run a nuclear plant, right up until the point something changed that would lead to a problem.

My email exchange with the General Manager makes clear to me that, in this case, Toyota's beautifully simple and successful approach to practical problem solving has not reached all the way to the end of its value stream – womb to tomb: the end where you and I have multiple contacts with the most customer-facing representatives of these automotive OEMs. This is snatching defeat from the jaws of victory of Roberto De Vicenzo proportions.

De Vicenzo, you will not be surprised to hear, never made the same mistake again. It is possible that I was unlucky enough to happen upon the one Toyota dealership that lacked formal problem-solving knowledge. But this is not the point. The point of relating this story is to ask *you* to look hard at your own business and ask whether you snatch defeat from the jaws of victory in any sense. It makes sense to start at the usual points of customer interface – quotation, sales, aftersales, service, warranty – and work backwards.

This problem occurred BEFORE Toyota's recent tough patch and I originally published this story as an article in 2009. Perhaps I experienced a taste of things to come. Certainly, Toyota would do well to reflect on this small slice of golf history.

Chapter 8

The Lean You - Personal responsibility

"It's difficult to wake someone who is pretending to be asleep"

8.1 Sensei, Sempai, Kohai

"Personal responsibility" may appear an obvious candidate for the list of key character traits of a 'successful' lean person. A part of me is inclined to agree, until I pull myself up short with the reminder that simply uttering the words does not fully convey the meaning or specific requirements - a bit like whispering to a friend, with an accompanying wink that "winning the lottery is easy, all you have to do is pick the right six numbers". The absence of practical guidance renders this a piece of accurate, but ultimately useless advice. So, I'll plough on give you my take on personal responsibility from three perspectives; my own experience, examples from both the world at large, and from within the lean settings.

These chapters entitled "The Lean You" can be read as a series of themes or traits shared by successful people in successful lean environments. Whilst the themes are common, the expression of each of the traits will differ from person to person. This chapter, covering "personal responsibility" is a good example. I have been fortunate to have three significant mentors in my working life, all of whom appear to possess remarkably similar belief systems but very different ways of expressing them.

The first of the three was Toshiyuki Muraoka, a Toyota Japanese veteran who trained me in the art of lean, TPS and trading him up into a better hotel room at no extra cost. Without ever uttering the two words, a good deal of his training was about personal responsibility. My time with him, whilst acutely painful at points, was fulfilling enough to spawn the name of my business; Sempai Consultancy Services. Sempai (sometimes expressed Senpai) is one half of a relationship equation that, upon discovery, felt very natural to me as a coaching style. The Sempai is the senior (not necessarily by age but by virtue of a combination of wisdom, skill and experience) with the Kohai taking a more "junior" but complementary role as the person being developed. The closest approximation, in a Western setting, is probably the mentor relationship.

Sempai : Kohai is even further removed from the traditional Boss : Subordinate relationship wherein lines of power are very clearly delineated. In Boss : Subordinate, at the risk of being simplistic, the Boss makes the big decisions and even though there is probably be a degree of consultation and passing on of knowledge, this does not underpin or serve as the raison d'être for the relationship. The Boss will likely harbour clandestine concerns about a well skilled subordinate who possesses the hungry eyes of one who covets the next step up to a bigger job. These are not ideal circumstances for the full development of the subordinate via the boss passing on everything he knows. Once again we arrive at turkeys, voting and the festive season.

The Sempai : Kohai relationship is founded on an alternative paradigm with clear, but unspoken, responsibilities on both sides. The Sempai must teach with clarity, at the correct pace for the Kohai to learn. Still, he must push the Kohai without breaking him. Testing the limits of the kohai's endurance without breaching them and giving freely of his knowledge are the dual traits of a seasoned Sempai. The Kohai must support the Sempai who willingly demonstrates his weaknesses, as well as his strengths, for the benefit of the Kohai's learning. The Kohai has a responsibility to learn as much as possible from the Sempai with a clear eye on the eventual goal of surpassing his Sempai.

This is how the knowledge base in society can grow. Note that the responsibility for learning in this relationship is at least 50:50. The learner must learn actively. He/she has personal responsibility. I received a harsh lesson on this point during my first kaizen workshop with Muraoka-san in Edinburgh. I was effectively the Kohai, supporting Nigel, my Sempai, at that point. Muraoka-san guided us both. Faced with a team of nine team members in a company that had paid many thousands of pounds for us to train them, I was to lead my first 5s activity.

Unsurprisingly it was rough around the edges but I received, what I felt to be, an undeservedly savage mauling in the customary end-of-the-day-hour-or-two review with the three of us and our interpreter. Perhaps I didn't help my cause by protesting "well it was my first time". This unexpectedly inflammatory comment enabled Muraoka-san to inform me, through a blushing interpreter, that this fact was irrelevant. Every time is the first time for the team I am teaching and there are no excuses. The first teaching is critical because it forms the base for future understanding.

On that day, I didn't agree (a fact that I judiciously kept quiet about) but I've long since come to agree with this sentiment in almost all circumstances. The net result being that my kids, in delicious moments of extreme exasperation, detest me. "It was my first time", whilst true, would have set in me a mindset to excuse myself too readily. The deeper lesson Muraoka-san conveyed was 'hansei', critical self-reflection.

8.2 Rugby, rules and TCUP

Dave Brailsford, discussed previously at length in the kodawari chapter, established a variation of the term "personal responsibility" along with trust, honesty and meticulousness, as one of his four key threads for sporting success. His term is "empowerment of athletes" whereby ownership of the training plan sits with each individual cyclist and group rules are set by the team, thus ticking the boxes for both personal and group ownership. Two for the price of one.

There are echoes of the approach taken by Sir Clive Woodward, supported by leadership expert and all-round bon viveur Humphrey Walters, to the long path which culminated in winning the Rugby World Cup in 2003. The English team were asked to set THEIR own rules; Woodward merely specified that there had to be some rules. In this respect, there appears to be a philosophical difference between Brailsford and Woodward on one side and Fabio Capello on the other. Capello is the current Manager of the English National Football Team who, before being parachuted in to rescue England from the "soft" management style endorsed by previous coach Steve McLaren, had a stellar career as a club manager. Capello is, by all accounts, anything but soft. HE instituted a number of rules early in 2008, laid out below for your enjoyment:

(1) Players agents, wives and girlfriends can no longer visit the team hotel

(2) Players can only use their mobile phones in their rooms

(3) Players cannot be late for meals and must now eat together

(4) Players cannot order room service

(5) Players must wear official England clothing at lunch and dinner

(6) Players must wear team blazers when in public

(7) Players are referred to by their surnames only, no nicknames

(8) Players cannot play their PlayStations

We could debate the rights and wrongs of these 8 rules, but this is not my point. I would argue that there is a lot to admire, in the detail, to aid the process of team bonding. Numbers 1 to 6 make sense to me. I can't get excited about number 7 which strikes me as unnecessarily draconian. A fair proportion of the male population would be casting their eyes toward The Hague to protest number 8 as a human rights infringement. This list, if compared to a Brailsford or a Woodward equivalent, would, I suspect, mirror theirs in many respects.

What, then, is the difference, if not in content? The answer is the source. This list is very much Capello's list and, early doors, it earned its corn by appearing to work very well. The team responded almost immediately and qualified in grand style for the South Africa hosted FIFA World Cup of 2010. Then something interesting happened as England, most fans and pundits would concur, badly underperformed during that tournament amidst quiet but persistent whispers of dressing room disquiet. Perhaps living for several weeks under rules that you had no part in creating is very different to tolerating them for the few days that characterise a "normal" national squad gathering. Certainly, the people operating in a lean business are together day after day where the cultural norms, if under-appreciated will quickly grate.

Another fine example of personal responsibility came to my attention only recently, although it stretches back several years. Incidentally, I ought to offer an apology for the frequent sporting references but sport provides a fascinating parallel competitive environment. It is no accident that some of the best sports people have, subsequently, been very successful in business.

A warm November night in Sydney, Australia, 2003 and an odd-shaped ball present a fine example. Rugby Union fans of an English persuasion have the date of November 22nd 2003 burned into their consciousness; the night that England beat Australia to win the Rugby World Cup in the Australians' back yard. Few tastes are sweeter to an English sports fan than this happy combination. The evening is largely remembered for the last-minute audacious drop goal from obsessive fly-half Jonny Wilkinson with only 26 seconds left on the clock. Those few seconds have generated thousands of column inches but we'll sidestep them and scamper onto something altogether more interesting.

Having said this, among the many thousands of hours of sporting commentary, very few moments linger long in the memory. I can think of only two. The first, from Kenneth Wolstenholme, when England went ahead 4-2 to win the 1966 Football World Cup:

"Some people are on the pitch...they think it's all over...it is now"

The second, from the lips of husky voiced Scotsman Ian Robertson, at the moment that Jonny Wilkinson secured the Rugby World Cup in 2003:

"He drops for World Cup glory. It's up! It's over! He's done it! Jonny Wilkinson is England's hero - yet again. And there's no time for Australia to come back. England have just won the World Cup."

And yet, my abiding memory of this day comes, not on the day, but seven years later when the England coach for that golden side, Sir Clive Woodward, appeared on BBC Radio 4's Desert Island Discs with Kirsty Young. Inevitably their conversation steered an early course to that night in Sydney and the final minute of the game.

His take, from pitchside, was slightly different as you might expect from the coach. Of course he remembers Jonny's drop goal but he was more pleased with the part played by all the men involved in that final manoeuvre. He collectively credits Wilkinson, Ben Kay, Steve Thomson and Lewis Moody with TCUP ability – 'Thinking correctly under pressure' - one of his central philosophies. Whilst obvious, it is pleasing when the head coach credits the team over the individual. This team had what the Japanese would call "wa", a deep consideration for team harmony. The team above the individual.

The intriguing part of the conversation covered the moments following the drop goal that give England a 20-17 lead. Woodward's view, in contrast to commentator Robertson's, was that there was indeed time for the Australians to come back.

For him, the dying moments were consumed by concern that the Australians would score from the re-start, a real risk given that the England players were, bar one, naturally distracted with minor celebrations and back-slapping. As Woodward remembers it, only one England player got himself back into the correct position immediately to respond to the Australian kick-off; Martin Johnson. The self-discipline (shitsuke) required for this simple act of personal responsibility is impressive.

There are many powerful expressions and examples of personal responsibility from the sporting arena; many of them more painful and far braver than Johnson's. I chose this one however as it combines several themes from this book - attention to detail (kodawari), focus and, the subject of this chapter "Personal Responsibility".

8.3 In the lean environment

So, how does this apply and why does it matter in a lean environment?

Consider the basics, 5s. It is now commonly known that the fifth "s" in the Japanese language is expressed as "shitsuke", the meaning of which tends to get lost in translation. Commonly our fifth "s" will be translated to become "sustain" or "custom and practice". The meaning is actually closer to self-discipline, not a million miles from the personal responsibility ascribed to Martin Johnson in the previous chapter.

Shitsuke is having the discipline to keep the area, tools and materials in good condition to allow us to work safely and productively by focusing on the job in hand; not having to compensate for something that is worn, broken, dirty, missing or badly placed.

Shitsuke is taking the tedious, and believe me it can be, personal responsibility of keeping the area in good condition during the shift and completing the 5s checks at the end of the shift - shift after shift after shift. Additionally, we have the under-appreciated gift that 5s bestows upon us beyond obvious safety and quality benefits; the ability to distinguish normal from abnormal. Of course seeing is just the beginning, we have to understand the possible consequence of what we are seeing (this is tricky as it's often an accumulation of the small things that tend to bite you on the backside, in a Three-Mile-Island-near-nuclear-meltdown or Challenger-shuttle-crash fashion).

Next we have to take personal responsibility to react, moreover react correctly, to these abnormalities including understanding WHEN to react immediately. Personal responsibility drives us to understand the standard, keep the standard, confirm the standard and react to the non-standard. My third mentor issued a regular, and simple, entreaty to his supervisors, managers and directors; "don't walk past poor safety, poor quality or poor productivity". He is now CEO of that $4bn business. Shitsuke goes way beyond 5s.

Almost all systems, no matter how simple, automated or well designed rely at some point on human intervention. We can force this intervention through rules and commandments but rules, counter-intuitively, have a limited impact. They are the jumping off point for control but the smart businesses aim to develop rules into common practices.

DENSO, for example, have codified and encouraged "Atarimae" or good habits that people develop and practice, as naturally as breathing, because they come to believe that they are the right thing to do. These range, at their simplest but most effective, from "not putting parts in a temporary home" or "not putting boxes of parts directly onto the floor" to "minimising the number of objects hanging from the ceiling" when designing a new facility to avoid giving people on the shop floor the oppressive feeling generated by a crowded ceiling.

There is clearly a management responsibility to show the reason and benefits of each atarimae but the basic principle is sound. A rule alone will be followed, generally, for fear of censure and can be guaranteed only if the boss is watching. An atarimae will occur whether the boss is there or not. It is truly voluntary, and makes sense as the boss can't be there all the time to watch everyone. We'd end up with top-heavy management ranks swollen in number to dwarf the value-added group on the shopfloor.

Even the small things matter. Let me rephrase that; the small things REALLY matter, especially if you are a business with a 5ppm Quality target from your customer. To grasp this, read Malcom Gladwell's fascinating book Outliers wherein he lays down some interesting ideas. A key one is that crises are "likely to be the result of an accumulation of minor difficulties and seemingly trivial malfunctions" rather than one significant "oops" moment.

The Three Mile Island partial core meltdown in Pennsylvania 1979 is a prime example, an unfortunate alignment of dark moons that led to the single biggest accident in the history of American commercial nuclear power generation. Those moons, each individually small and avoidable were a blockage in the plant's polisher, **compounded by** the valves for the backup system being shut, **compounded by** an indicator in the control room showing they were closed being blocked by a repair tag hanging from a switch above it, **compounded by** the second backup system, a relief valve, not working properly that day, either. It stuck open when it was supposed to close, **compounded by** a gauge in the control room (which should have told the operators that the relief valve wasn't working) not working. The Three Mile Island radiation leak would not have happened if ANY one of these incidents - dark moons - had not aligned.

You get the point. Gladwell reports that the President's commission investigating the events concluded, simplistically, that human error was the problem. A counter-argument can be made that the management system was broken and did not ensure that the correct, critical items were confirmed at the right time in the right way, by the right person.

Over to the lean factory. Let's consider a serious defect flowing out to the Customer. Whenever I have investigated these in the past I have rarely seen one big failure at the root of the problem. Generally, several small ones like Standardised Work not being followed **compounded by** a neighbour check not being done **compounded by** a poka-yoke device being over-ridden **compounded by** a cell patrol not being performed by a supervisor led to the defect. All chances to prevent, spot, contain and correct the problem were squandered.

Perhaps this is the Brailsford, Woodward, Capello line of thinking. If we couple attention to detail with personal responsibility we start to get a feel for a strong way of working, assuming that we don't try to confirm everything. The skill is to identify and confirm the critical conditions and variables that are most likely to give us a problem; otherwise we'd all go out of business from the cost of an army of checkers irrespective of how visual we make our factory.

This is the basis of previously mentioned Jikoutei-Kanketsu (Built-in Quality with ownership), a management system built on personal responsibility and kodawari.

I harbour longstanding concerns that, at least in British society, we slowly erode the importance of personal responsibility. Tracing a path from post war children, through baby-boomers, generation X and into generation Y sees a blurring of the lines between childhood and adulthood. Perhaps age is catching up with me but I see a generation not so keen on taking responsibility; the Government is always at fault or it's somebody else's fault.

A small example. I remember taking my children, as toddlers, to birthday parties and watching open mouthed during pass-the-parcel as EVERY child had to have a turn to win and EVERY layer of paper peeled away to reveal a prize. Is this an entirely useful way of encouraging resilience in our children? If the dice-rolling of life means that sometimes you lose, it's a useful skill to be able to pick yourself up and move on. 'Nana korobi ya oki' - fall down seven times, get up eight.

Often my 8 year old chooses not to wear a coat, even when the rain is sheeting in sideways. I can't expect him to decide whether his parents should put their mortgage on a fixed rate or float with the Bank of

England base rate, but he does know the impact of not taking a coat on a cloudy day. If he chooses not to, well, it's a learning opportunity.

Flexibility, Clear Thinking and Personal Responsibility are the 3 key skills that I have chosen to cover in this book. There are many others to acquire on the pathway to mastery. I can only recommend that you follow the advice of Malcolm Gladwell and be sure to get your 10,000 hours worth of practice in.

Finally, before we move to the wise words of my Sensei, Muraoka-san, remember that top figure skaters fall over more in practice than average ones. Pick the bones out of that!

Chapter 9

The Sensei view - Reflections of a Toyota veteran

"He who chops his own wood warms himself twice"

9.1 On...working at Toyota in the 1960's

As a final chapter I wanted to offer you something a little different by way of an interview with the man I consider my sensei.

Toshiyuki Muraoka has something of an advantage over many in that he worked in Japan for Toyota for 34 years from the 1960s to the 1990s. Crucially, he worked in the Kamigo plant, which was one of the breeding and experimentation grounds for the formulation of the Toyota Production System (TPS); indeed, his path was regularly crossed by Taichi Ohno. What sets him apart is that he has the unique perspective of this background married to a decade of consulting to UK-based companies. Thus he understands our woes with the clarity of one who has trodden a better path.

I worked with Muraoka-san for 14 months continuously in the late 1990s, at the SMMT Industry Forum, where he had a dramatic and long-lasting effect upon all of the engineers he trained hands on. Occasionally I am still jolted from my sleep with the memory of his painfully harsh but fruitful training. We keep in touch and he agreed to be interviewed through our favourite interpreter.

By the way, some of the grammar may jar a little but I have purposely remained faithful to Muraoka-san's words as interpreted. To tinker with the phrasing loses some of the essence and would dilute the message. Occasionally I have inserted square bracketed words [ ] to clarify points or enable sentences to flow better. I should be clear that the wood-chopping title of this chapter is my suggestion. It encapsulates, in my view, a lot of what Muraoka-san discusses below.

We spent some time looking backwards at his Toyota background and some time looking forward at the challenges facing the UK and global businesses. Our discussion was wide ranging and below are some excerpts.

Thank you for joining me today, Muraoka-san. Could you start by telling us about your Toyota background?

I joined Toyota in the year of the Tokyo Olympics, 1964 and started my career in the Motomatchi plant, in the transmissions section and the milling machine was my work. The Motomatchi plant made engines, transmissions and bodies. In those days it was the motorisation era of Japan and the automobile was going like hot pies. In those days the Publica, Crown and Corolla were the three types of cars in the Motomatchi plant.

The people in Toyota had started to look into customers' preferences because there was space only for three different models so you had to specialise in certain models. Two years later I moved to the engine plant area of the Kamigo plant making the M-type engine and the head transfer machine was my particular area. The transfer machines started to appear gradually but in those days the Japanese manufacturing machinery didn't expand to this type of machine as the UK, US and Germany had the skill and the knowledge [of] those technologies.

Somebody upstairs was thinking we cannot continue like this and we have to develop our own transfer machines. The first Toyota designed prototype machine came into my area. It was actually manufactured by Toshiba [but] because it was new, the quality was not right and the machine was failing here and there. The customers were looking for more and more cars but because of the poor quality of the machine we were always mending it. When the machine was working beautifully you just produce more and more and more.

In the engine plant there were several different subassemblies – piston lines, head lines, crank shaft, cylinder block, which then go into the assembly area. If any part of the subassembly was missing nothing was produced along the assembly line and so that was the chance for the remaining machines, that hadn't failed, to pile up safety stock. That was my daily survival of not being chased by the assembly line and it was like that for several years until Mr Ohno came to the Kamigo plant with Mr Suzumura, a very fat guy.

[Author's note: Muraoka-san tells several stories about Ohno-san and Suzumura-san, including an instance where Suzumura purposely would damage parts they had made in advance (in case of breakdown) to ram home the message of overproduction waste.]

Everybody knew that the machine was no good and tended to fail and they were asking us 'What's wrong with this machine, what part is wrong, how does it stop?' but being an operator you couldn't explain why. I now remember that everything I said about why it failed were only excuses. The machine is not right or the repairer didn't do a good job last time. These are the excuses to say 'I am doing fine, there is nothing wrong with me' and as a result you never think about how to improve.

Then the company started to talk about improving things, it was like a competition. You describe what you think should be done to improve the situation and then if your idea is good and usable you get money. Anybody was qualified to have ideas whether in an office area or shop floor.

9.2 On...training at Toyota

How did Toyota train you in TPS? [Muraoka-san eventually rose to become a highest rank TPS instructor.]

After five years of joining the company you can attend the initial course of TPS. That's simply the basic method of how to deal with kanbans or understanding standard operations. It was almost compulsory, if you wanted to keep your job you had to attend this course. The course was broken into two-hour or three-hour courses here and there. So going through this experience of attending and learning how to think you gradually get educated and started to practice because everybody has learnt the same thing. Everybody in Toyota is transformed one way or another to become better personnel. So anyway, as I said, the automobile industry was growing very fast in that period. The Celica came in and the Corolla went all over the world not just within Japan and QC Circle type activities [were] started to reduce rejects. My group's QC Circle activity got the top prize in the plant, then district and then all over Toyota Kamigo and in those days there were 3,000 people in Kamigo.

You [had to] go to the HQ to give a presentation of what you have done so it gradually became recognised that I was good at those things. I became a Team Leader (TL), then promoted to Group Leader (GL) and then Assistant Manager.

These roles were generally five years long for you?

I believe in the need to stick with something for five years to gain full knowledge and that again is Toyota's idea of career management. When I learned TPS for the first time they didn't talk about technical things, the functions of this and that, it's not touched upon. It's the method of how you work with those components or how to use your people, also how to use the bosses. Those are the things that you learn through TPS.

So, gradually, a part of TPS is how to fill the gap of your knowledge. The GL looks at the TLs under him and has to make sure that these TLs will be eventually replacing himself as GL. You have to educate them. You should always be prepared to be moved away. The TL has to be a deputy to you asap. Anyway that's how Toyota thinks. You can't say 'I know this, but I'm not going to tell you'. Sometimes you might yourself take an interest in a different area and if your TL is capable of standing in then you can go and study it. Also your boss will be looking at you and thinking 'Ah, he can leave his position and that means he's educated his team leader already' and that's to your benefit.

Teaching is one thing but let them practice alone. You have to leave and let him do it to identify where he still has to learn. If the TL is able to replace the GL [that means] he's got certain knowledge and practice behind him already. So that is the sustainability. If you want to be promoted you have to make sure you are not needed there because the next person is already there.

What were the significant things you learned from Toyota that made you ready to come to the UK to pass on TPS?

Quite candidly I didn't choose to come to the UK but was sent. In a Japanese company you don't have freedom of what you are going to do next. However, when this invitation or order comes you can take two approaches: just hate it but do it or try to like it and do it. Mr Ohno's idea about this is that the good idea is the product of your tight corner, so that's the spirit when you are going through hell.

I knew it was going to be upheaval because I didn't know anything about the UK or the language but something I knew was the very poor competitiveness of the UK and European manufacturing industry. I knew that all that I had been doing in Toyota was to develop the people coming behind me where, as a result, the QCDP was excellent (but not just a [lucky] by-product). Education was and is the primary target so when I came to the UK to train you and the other engineers, I knew I would be doing exactly what I had been doing [in Toyota Japan]. I thought 'Well OK, it's not that bad.'

You have been in the UK for 10 years now. I started with you two years after you first arrived and heard stories about how frustrated you were when you first came to the UK? What are your reflections on those first few years?

They [engineers, managers] spoke too much as if that's how they earned money. It was almost like competing with each other about how much you could talk and that's how you should conduct the business! When you look at what they had actually achieved, because they were busy talking, nothing had been done. You know that at least the production line is making things, whether they are faulty or not, they are at least making things. Two engineers would be talking without looking and I would challenge, 'What did you learn from the line?' and they gave no good answer, and that stupid answer frustrated me.

Is this style of harsh teaching a Japanese style or a Toyota style?

You see the harder you try the feeling of success is greater at the end, so that's why I wanted you to go through a hard patch. In Japan the teaching environment is to let YOU think. When you hear something, rather than [just] absorbing it you have to think, 'Why is he saying that?'

and then you have to practise that and the penny drops sometimes. I feel maybe the British process of teaching is different from this. The answer is too readily available. [It should be that] if you don't think of a good question nobody will tell you.

In order to have a question you have to think so if you want to learn something about the shop floor you have to go through a difficult phase. Like a professional footballer does not perform well from reading instructions. Maybe he does that as well but they are mainly on the field practising and learning from their body without thinking how they should react.

9.3 On...consultants and the Management responsibility

Do you have the same concerns for UK competitiveness now?

It is very weak. I've never actually formally assessed but it's not getting better. Now maybe the Japanese plants in the UK are getting ok but if you go to the purely UK supplier plants things are not really turning better. Maybe one of the reasons is that they are not really good at using their budget to the best. Sometimes they are calling consultants thinking that spending money on the consultant itself is going to do the trick rather than analysing what is the weak point of the company and then call in the consultant for a specific purpose. So that means that the consultant can do whatever they want to do and say change this or change that.

Is this a management failure of not looking hard enough?

You see they don't have a big picture or a detailed picture and are just in the middle beating the bush [a reference to randomly trying to scare birds out of the undergrowth during shooting season]. The question is where to start. First of all the bottom up is very important – the working people have to be encouraged but the top down is also important because they have to guide which way to go.

When you analyse the weakness you have to create the plan and [decide] when to call in the consultant to deal with this or that. For that reason the top and the bottom have to co-operate with each other to understand the real state of the health of the company. To do that you have to always forget about your high pride that you are doing fine; 'Where are you failing?' is the question. Forget that you've got a PhD in this or that or 15 years of experience here. Just look at things in a very candid manner.

If you decide to call in a consultant you have to put good confidence in the consultant rather than, 'I will take this part of the advice but I won't take this.' Like when you worked in SMMT you had full confidence in me 100%. You may not understand exactly what I wanted to do but you had confidence that somehow I am trying to do good. But of course you have to assess that a consultant is worth putting your confidence in by looking into his background, what he has been doing. Whether he has worked on the shop floor in his own career or finished university, went into one of the Toyota plants and then became a consultant.

Quite often when a university graduate works in a leadership function and an improvement activity has taken place, the people on the shop floor have been working hard to make it happen but the university graduate thinks that that's what HE has done, but he didn't.

This is maybe my guidance to assess the good consultant. The people who used to work on the shop floor are much kinder to people on the shop floor and therefore, when that leader has got the idea that QCD has to be improved, his sentiment is much more easily understood by the people who have to do that. What tends to happen in the UK plant is that managers tend not to look at [shop floor] processes to align their approach to the shop floor issues that the operator deals with. Therefore the operator on the shop floor feels exploited as work is made harder and it cannot be sustained.

Consider many young consultants, after learning for a while they know the theory and the calculations. [But] they have no background experience on the shop floor. They know how the formula works and they can teach it but we have to always understand why something is poor right now (quality or whatever) and know that on that knowledge you can build the development. If this is missing then the methodology does not produce results. So this applies to Japan as well where some managers and engineers get in the company because of the big university brand name behind them, but when they are standing beside the shop floor machine, the machine doesn't see their university name! But, the people on the shop floor who have far less qualifications, the machine knows them because those people touch the machine. It is very important for those people who know the machines (and are known by the machines) to be developed further to manage the machines and the people.

But of course that alone wouldn't do the trick because you always need some kind of innovation that comes from outside. You can build improvements so much but big pushes come from innovation and that's where you need university people. But they have to come into the shop rather than the other way round and hopefully that will be a good arrangement for the company to develop and prosper. So a lot of top graduates in the offices don't understand the shop floor or they don't have a common language with the shop floor.

We have to be always listening and trying to understand what the business wants to achieve. As a consultant you talk with the managers and they will give you their problems. You then observe the shop floor and you have to match these two stories: the treasure on the shop floor and the manager's worry. Then you identify the area which delivers a good result for the manager and the business. You have to be very good at this. This is the skill of the consultant.

What do you think of the UK Government strategy to support industry – too much, too little?

It's not really aligned to the real thing. What they are thinking about trying to achieve is good but I'm not quite sure that those policies are to benefit their own political happiness or for a better Britain as a whole. It will be very difficult to change that because the politician has his own frame of mind to work in. The two countries [Japan and the UK] are in a similar environment. Small island countries with materials from abroad which we process and sell, a very similar structure. So considering that standpoint we should be able to come up with a better industrial organisation rather than just the financial sector being the big earner. We have to really think, 'How is this country going to earn its living in the future?' A lot of industry is transferring manufacturing capability to China and you lose your manufacturing base. In order to survive we have to add more value to our own products.

9.4 On...the future

For a young manager reading this article what would be the one strong piece of advice you would give them for the future?

You see human beings have got two eyes, two ears and two nostrils. In Japan, the sacred people are in the Buddhist religion. 'Sacred people' when written in the Kanji alphabet [one of the three Japanese alphabets] looks like a mouth and ear. The ear is a lot bigger letter than the mouth. The sacred people learn to always listen before they speak: a small amount of talking is sufficient. Basically the mouth is for eating. So the ears, eyes, nose are there to tell you primarily the danger around our environment. That's why we have these organs.

An old Japanese story tells of a very clever person in ancient times that could allegedly listen to 10 people speaking at the same time and deliver the answer to those 10 people without making a mistake. So, those are the people we respected very highly in Japan. So if you are talking too much then you are not thinking.

Listen and do it and if you give it a try, assess whether the result was as expected. When you are a manager and instruct other people to do certain things, go back and ask whether it worked. If it didn't or did, what is the next step you are going to give to them? That is the education. If it's good, do it better, analyse. Like I was saying earlier, my first five years in Toyota I wasn't told about TPS.

The first course was delivered in the fifth year and the intermediate course was delivered five years after that and after 30 years I got the top class TPS training. So learning TPS is following a similar process to when you went to elementary, secondary school and university in this order –

and that is going through a development process. Now my feeling is that a number of companies employ people and instead of delivering the first and second course they just go straight into the university degree course. One step at a time; education takes time. You can't have a very short quick result. If you do that you are missing the process.

Is the big difference between the UK and Japan that Japan had to rebuild after the war?

You see our generation were in a sense united together because we had to really come out of a crash and start again so everybody was trying very hard. Our generation thought, 'How is Japan going to survive like this?' and [was] talking about how to feed the family, how to make Japan prosper but the young generation is only thinking about me. Rather than thinking about their career [in post-war Japan] they just made it happen. Then the next generations don't have a united goal like this. Everybody starts to chase their own dreams. We shouldn't spoil ourselves with things. We have to think how to do that.

Is this one of the few positive sides of a recession?

Underdeveloped countries are trying always very hard to catch up and have a good life. When the benefit of the nation is exactly the same as the benefit for myself that's fine but when it does not match it's a problem. Look at history, no country which has climbed to the height of the world has ever retained that position – the Roman Empire, the Egyptian Empire, etc. Up to that point they had been fighting, fighting to achieve a goal. Once it's achieved they collapse. In a similar way the company should be viewed. How you align what is good for the company with what is good for the operators and everybody else in the company is a big question.

Eiji Toyoda helped steer Toyota for 50 years – how did he stay hungry and keep Toyota improving?

It's not really one person's doing. You remember that Toyota went bankrupt once so that, in a sense, was the start point of the current Toyota company. At one point Toyota was in receivership to the bank and that was when I joined. Mr Nakagawa was the president of the Toyota Company but he was seconded from the bank. Eiji Toyoda was the third position below him. Within 10 years we were returned to a normal operation. During that period everybody thought, 'never again bankruptcy' and TPS is based on that kind of resilient spirit.

But the DNA was really started by the founder of the Toyota loom Sakichi Toyoda. He observed his mother using an old traditional loom and every so often she found a defect in the weaving and had to undo up to that point and then tie the thread. He just felt, 'That's a pity that she has to destroy good work to go back to that point,' and he devised a way that the machine would stop when a thread snapped. He visited the USA where a machinery exhibition was taking place, stayed there two months and studied all the modern machinery and because he was a carpenter [in those days looms were an all-wooden structure] he was very good at changing pieces here and there. That was because he just wanted to help his mother.

That's the DNA of TPS. The idea comes out by observing, so what I always say is don't hide the problems. Expose the problems [because] when the problems become serious everybody starts to think. So maybe a lot of companies, in the loom situation, would have said, 'Repair it or make a new one' but the spirit in Toyota is to observe where is it failing and ask can we do something about it. Now we use the words 'seven wastes' to demonstrate it more easily but we really need to educate operators and everybody else to observe and think. [This means] the way you look at things and what questions you should have in your mind when you are observing. That is the teaching.

So that's why, in Toyota the first banner the new recruit sees on the wall, and is taught, is 'good product, good thinking'. Now because good thinking is nailed in from the very beginning you have to come up with the ideas when you are working like, 'Is this the best way?' or 'How can I stop this awkward work?' So that is good thinking. [We had talked earlier about suggestion schemes – not included in the text and he referred back to it here.] Rewarding suggestions is a kind of forward investment. You give 500 yen at this point in time and the company gets the crop out of it at a later point when the company needs it. So even when the work is hard you know that somebody on the line has earned 500 yen that has to be paid back somehow!

You see I remember Rousseau said that the human being is just a reed in the wind but it is a thinking reed. Flimsy and weak but we have a brain. You have to use this thinking resource but you shouldn't really force people to do it. You have to coax them to do it as a part of daily life. The idea may not work but the habit of him thinking will be a benefit. You don't need to practise, just come up with the idea and you get 500 yen.

For example if the boss thinks that Russell who has had a 500-yen idea has got something about him he may think, 'He will be a team leader in three years' time.' Also now [that] your idea is incorporated you think, 'Have I got any more ideas?' So that's natural. That's how Toyota teach you to think. Those are the experiences I had. You see there's an iron rule; when the operator comes up with an improvement idea it has a 100% success rate because they know what they are talking about. The critical part is that somebody has to say, 'OK, do it.'

When I am leading an improvement activity I don't generate any ideas, the ideas come from them and that is the secret of success. That's a kind of management skill where it's quite important to let them think that they did it. If it doesn't work it's not a failure, just analyse why. Don't say, 'Why did you do that?' We have to say, 'Why did it fail?' That's the way they start to learn how to analyse. Usually I can direct which area to look at to see why it didn't work based on my own experience.

A Final Word

As you might expect, I have read and corrected this book repeatedly during the editing process. Of the nine chapters, the final one containing Muraoka-san's words never loses its lustre and serves to remind that I am several decades from reaching his level - if I work hard, with a following wind. In less charitable moments I would argue that he 'cheated' by (i) being born in Japan (ii) during Toyota's growth / experimentation years and (iii) staying for 34 years.

By way of a final note, around 1999 I searched long and hard for some kind of algorithm for lean implementation. I desperately desired a paint-by-numbers solution to avoid the inadequacy I frequently felt of not knowing where to start or exactly where the finish was.

Please don't waste your time like I did; there is no master algorithm. Sure, there are guidelines and sensible paths but no one-size-fits-all answer. I hope this book goes some way to showing the need to understand the challenges collectively facing us, strengthening our businesses to deal with them, and developing the personal behaviours to survive and thrive.

If, on the other hand, you fancy the master algorithm search, the small story below is for you. Enjoy staring into the pool.

"In the forest there is a pool and in the pool there are three golden carp. One lists and swims in downward circles. Soon he lies weightless on the bottom sand, and he is relished by the water snails who want to live as he did. On the surface and under an undulating lily pad, dart five golden babies protected by the mother carp and threatened by the hungry father carp. Two of these escape and grow to maturity and themselves make

young. One of these lives to a grand old age because he has been clever in sneaking babies away from their mothers. 'But,' he tells himself, 'I have made the swift ones swifter.'

Now, each day for many years, a boy has lain here looking into the depths of the pool and watching the countless little golden generations. Knowing that none have left the pool, he stares into the water and asks a passionate question:

How many fish are in this pool!"

The Ronin, William Dale Jennings

About the Author

Russell Watkins is a director of Sempai Consultancy Services, a business formed to assist organisations that are serious about improving the short and long-term performance of their business. He has held various operations, materials and lean manufacturing positions within the automotive, aerospace and construction industries. He first experienced the harsh training of Toyota Japanese engineers in the 1990s, and his work since has taken him to businesses – shopfloors and boardrooms – throughout the UK, Europe, the US, China, India, Japan and South America.

Russell Watkins can be contacted by email: russell@sempai.co.uk

Web site: www.sempai.co.uk

Twitter: @leansempai

Lightning Source UK Ltd.
Milton Keynes UK
UKOW051138280312

189749UK00001B/164/P